Empire of Liberty

Empire of Liberty

Tom Donelson

iUniverse, Inc.
New York Lincoln Shanghai

Empire of Liberty

iUniverse, Inc.

For information address:
iUniverse, Inc.
2021 Pine Lake Road, Suite 100
Lincoln, NE 68512
www.iuniverse.com

ISBN: 0-595-30589-X

Printed in the United States of America

Contents

BOOK III: The New South: A Reappraisal.

BOOK IV: Thoughts on God

BOOK V: A Few More Thoughts

Book VI: Conservatism Revisited

Acknowledgements

I have many friends to thank for this book. First of all, my editor Carol Golden, whose tireless effort and editing made this book possible, and Kim Smith for her help in designing the cover. Both of these ladies have been with me since the inception of my publishing company and have been involved in every book that I have written. My friendship with Carol goes back even further.

Over the past year, I discussed many of the issues in this book with many individuals including my children, Kat and Bethany, as well as Frank Lotierzo, and Richard Nadler. My debates and discussions with these individuals helped shaped the book and sharpen my arguments. Not all of these individuals agree with me but I value their advice and friendship. And in the case of my daughters, their love.

I want to thank my daughters Bethany and Kat, as well as Carol Golden, for their help in occasional research, as well as Michele Catalina and Evelyn Forsythe for their cooperation in selected chapters.

Finally, I want to thank my wife for her patience and willingness to allow me to pursue my dreams, and of course, my parents for their love and their teaching.

Introduction

The world has changed, and for the past year, I have taken the liberty to write selected essays, some of which have been published about the events shaping this world. I also decided to discuss those individuals who have helped shape the present world that exists today through their courage and ideas. Whitaker Chambers was a witness to the horror that was communism. A man beset with guilt and a born again Christian, Chambers told the world the truth about the nature of communism. Very few people know Chambers today but his proclamation of the truth short circuited his career and shortened his life. Just as he was becoming a leading voice in American journalism, his admission of his communist past and his battle against Alger Hiss ended his career. It also put a severe strain on his heart. Even after his days at Time magazine ended though, his contribution to freedom continued through his book, *Witness,* and various pieces for the fledging new journal, *National Review.* The irony was that when Chambers left the Communist Party, he thought he was joining the losing side. He never lived to see the final implosion of communism.

F.A. Hayek was for many years a lone voice in the academic world on the validity of the free market, and even today very few of us know his work or his name, though his ideas and theories triumphed. The Great Depression supposedly ended free market as an idea, but Hayek maintained that it would be communism and socialism that would fail. Even in the depth of the Depression, Hayek maintained his faith in capitalism. He was right.

Leslie Groves was the man behind the Atomic Bomb project. His management skills and his abilities were as instrumental in getting the Manhattan project completed as the scientific skills required to make it work. What would happen if Nazi Germany or the Soviet Union had obtained the bomb first? History would have been different and not for the best. Groves saw to it that America was first.

The opening essay is the heart of the book and represents my argument on the need for a new foreign policy. America stands alone as the new superpower, feared as much as admired. Many leaders throughout the world view American foreign policy as an attempt to establish worldwide hegemony and truly fear an American revolutionary zeal for change. While we may view the present administration as "conservative"—to an Arab principality or maybe to the leaders of the present Chinese government—American ideals represent a threat to their power. This essay was inspired by the various debates that I held with many of those on the political left between 1984 and 1991. The one aspect that comes into play was that the ideas that I defended in those debates proved to be correct. I will suggest that my ideas are still correct today. America is a force for good. American Ideals are triumphing throughout the world, and yet opposition to those ideas is still there. From the various cells of radical Islamic fundamentalists to various intellectual elites in Europe and even in the United States, America is still attacked with both words and bullet. Just ask yourself this, would the world be better if the United States was not active in world affairs? That is the heart of the debate. My view is simple. America is good for the world.

BOOK I

Empire of Liberty

Editor's note: A few years back, I had the opportunity to debate John Swomley, a leading left activist on the First Gulf War. Dr. Swomley wrote a book in 1970, titled "American Empire." His point was that America was not a force for good. My point was and still is the opposite. The United State's role in the world is for good.

1

The Prologue

It is the year 2003 and the United States stands as the pivotal power in the world, with the opportunity to establish an Empire of Liberty. We are not talking the typical empire of controlling territory but an empire based upon the spread of ideas—ideas of liberty. The ascendancy of the United States extends into science, technology, popular culture, and its military is becoming a force for stability. When the Balkans exploded in violence in the 1990's, it was the American military that brought order to the region as Europeans proved incapable of establishing order even in their own backyard. Throughout the past two decades, the United States has become the guarantor of democracy worldwide and in some cases, the judge of the fairness of foreign elections.

Throughout the world, the American military stands prepared from Central Europe to the DMZ in Korea. Until September 11th, 2001, American preeminence was treated with indifference and in some cases fear from its own populace. During the past three presidential elections, domestic concerns dominated and serious foreign policy issues never made the front burners in the electorate mind. Suddenly, America found itself in a war of terror after over 3,000 Americans and foreign nationals (from over 85 other countries) were killed in suicide attacks, and foreign policy suddenly became important once again just as it was in the Cold War.

There are critics both on the right and the left that fear this development and there are others who are tying to debate what policies need to be followed. Those who fear this development range from Pat Buchanan's xenophobic vision of America to various members of the old left, who still rate America as the sole evil in the world. The Buchanan vision is based on old style conservative isolationist views that declare that the world will corrupt America. The old Left takes the opposite tack; America will corrupt the world with its consumer economy and its military adventures.

Pat Buchanan used to be a defender of free trade and America's role in world affairs, but after leaving the Reagan administration, Buchanan joined many on the left in opposing both Gulf War I and free trade. Mr. Buchanan once remembered a conversation with a friend, "As America was defying the Soviets with little help and less gratitude from those we were defending, I muttered to a friend about our "ungrateful allies." "What other kind are there?" he retorted."

Buchanan compare America's foreign policy in the 19th century with that of the 20th century when he wrote in his magazine, *The American Conservative*, "And in making an alliance with the mortal enemy of our Mother Country, we were putting America's interests first....In every foreign war of the 19th century, U.S. presidents did the same. In 1812, we declared war on Britain when she was in a death struggle with Napoleon, in the hope of seizing Canada. In 1846, we declared war on Mexico to keep Texas and seized the Southwest. In 1898, McKinley was stampeded into war over Cuba but made the best of it by annexing Puerto Rico, the Philippines, and Hawaii." Of course, Buchanan misses the irony that many of the wars he mentioned were foreign adventures and as Max Boots observed in his book, *Savage Wars of Peace*, America has been involved in foreign wars even in the "isolationist" 19th century. In the Jefferson Administration, the United States waged war against the Barbary Pirates—our first combat in the Middle East. The result of the war as Max Boots noted, "The naval operations had established an important principle—freedom of the seas—and helped end for all time the threat to commercial shipping from the corsairs."

Buchanan declares himself a nationalist and "believes in the Old Republic." Buchanan's theory is to use the nationalist movement as a wedge issue to build a "new conservative moment" in which the working middle class blue collar rebellion is the basis of a new center-right" coalition. As author Richard Nadler observed in his book, *Perils of Pat*, "In Buchanan's world, where autarky is ideal, trade—a form of war—is an impediment...If free trade is an impediment, then the presence or absence of institutions which promote it—private property rights civil liberties, constitutional restraints on government—are geopolitically nugatory." Nadler's point is that for Buchanan, promoting economic freedom has ceased to be a goal and as Nadler comments, "Different strokes for different folks, says Pat. Arabs, for instance, adore dictators who gas villagers, set tanks on enclaves of religious dissidents, practice mass impressments for suicidal wars, and torture ordinary citizens with the apparatus of a police state. They love Saddam, says Pat. That's their culture. Buchanan is a global multiculturalist."

While some Libertarians and Buchanan believe that a Fortress America would save America money, Nadler notes that the price of "Economic isolationism yields global depression. Political isolationism—non-response to aggression—enhances the market value of raw force. A strategy that leads inevitably to war won't reduce defense outlays." Pay me now or pay me later. Nadler declares, "The loss of freedom anywhere diminishes its prospects everywhere, and each gain helps to secure our liberties." To be a free trader is to be a nationalist. To support a strong American presence will enhance liberty worldwide.

The reverse is that to have allowed Saddam to develop a nuclear presence, and strengthen his chemical or biological capacity would have weakened America's position in a crucial area. As Nadler asked, "Would America be likelier to support armed action against a nuclear power?" Certainly becoming a nuclear power allows North Korea to engage in blackmail and extortion demands for financial aid that permits the regime's survival.

Conservative critics' fail to accept the seriousness of the international threat and also fail to understand that Americans (even from this nation's inception) did in fact engage in foreign adventures. From the "Halls of Montezuma to the shores of Tripoli" demonstrate that Americans fought foreign wars to defend their national interest and most of these conflicts were undeclared. Certainly, we are not talking conquest of foreign lands or establishing colonies like the British, but we are saying that America is the leading defender of freedom today. While the conservative isolationist movement is based on the idea of world corruption on American values, their mirror image on the left believes the exact opposite-It is America that corrupts the world.

John Swomley, a leading leftist for the past half-century, based his entire career on this ideal. His 1970 tome, "American Empire", presented a world in which the Soviet Empire and the United States resembled two Scorpions in a bottle—both were equally guilty. For the past decade, John Swomley has promoted détente with North Korea and been critical of our South Korean allies. Swomley declared the South Korean economy being "completely dominated by foreign capital. All the major Korean firms were built either with foreign loans or joint investments with foreign capitalists [chiefly U.S and Japanese]" This opinion explains Swomley's attitude toward America's role in international economy. For Swomley, American involvement in the world economy is exploitive. Somehow, the progress of the South Korean economy going from extreme poverty to a developed status within one generation escapes Swomley. South Korea's economy was built from investments from the United States and Japan just as the United States was built from British investments in the 19th century. In order for third world countries to advance, they must be part of the international economy. Free trade enhances third world countries economic vitality in the long run, and studies have shown that countries that have a strong judicial system, low taxes, and low tariff barriers tend to have higher economic prosperity. North Korea's autarky system has produced a one-million man military and massive poverty and starvation for the average North Korean, whereas, South Korea is a country dominated by a growing middle class.

In 1970, Swomley wrote, "The surest way to prevent the spread of communism and provide long-range advantage to the U.S. economy is by *ending the present foreign policy of anti-Communism based on American military and business control of other countries.*" Yet, by ignoring Swomley's advice, the United States did win the cold war with Russia now becoming slowly integrated with the West. In a 1990 debate about the Gulf War with this author, Swomley still was declaring America a loser in the Cold War—a country exhausted by the obligation of Empire and bankrupt by the Cold War military spending. This in the middle of the longest peacetime expansion in America's history! Over the next decade, America continued a two-decade economic expansion. Swomley still is opposing the war on terrorism and still declaring that America is exploiting Third World nations. Swomley summarized his position when he concluded in his book, "Neither the United States nor the Soviet Union today offers real hope to the world for peace or freedom or justice. The power of attraction that will move men down these roads must therefore come from the minorities in both nations and in other nations, who will not be seduced by the call to war or by the rewards of political conformity, but who will lead in social criticism, and social change." Swomley considered American voters naïve and sheep-like in following a different path than what he recommended. He was wrong and the average American voter who supported a strong American military presence proved to be correct. The left's opposition to America's new role has been compromised for being on the wrong side of history for the past 50 years. When they offered appeasements, romantic idealism about our enemies and half way measures of defense—their solutions were proven wrong. When the Berlin Wall came crashing down in 1989 and the Soviet Empire finally collapsed in 1991, the left's view of foreign policy came crashing down with it. While the Left is still strong in many academic centers, the American people have long since rejected their ideals.

2

Cost of Empire

Throughout the 19th century, Great Britain ran an Empire that was worldwide. Scholar Alvin Rabushka wrote, "The most remarkable achievement in the economic transformation of nineteenth-century Britain was a steady reduction in government spending from 1815 to 1890." Throughout the 18th century, Great Britain were involved in various European and world wars. The French and Indian War along with the American Revolution was a worldwide conflict and the century concluded with a major European armed explosion starting with the French Revolution and concluding with Napoleon's defeat at Waterloo.

After Waterloo, Great Britain was bankrupt and a country whose domestic policy was based on mercantilist policy that included excessive government regulations and taxes. The biggest items of government spending after the Napoleonic Era was debt interest, military spending and local government spending on poor relief. In 1811, total government spending was 27.1 percent of gross national income and by 1890, the total was down to 7.3 percent. Great Britain began a century of enacting low taxes, free trade and stable monetary policy and the result was a dramatic increase of prosperity throughout Great Britain. With wages rising sharply, the working class saw their income doubled in the last half of the century and a new middle class emerged.

Great Britain managed to maintain an Empire with a "Laissez-faire" free market policy, which included lowering tax rates—similar to the debate going on in Washington now as Congress debates whether to lower marginal tax rates while increasing military spending. Max Boots, in his book "Savage War of Peace", stated, "Contrary to the dreams of some economic determinists, capitalism and freedom do not spread inexorably on their own. The nineteenth-century free trade was protected and expanded by the Royal Navy." Britain battled pirates and slave traders, and the British Navy extended protection to the world's oceans.

America faces equivalent tasks including battling terrorists, narco-traffickers as well as Regional military powers.

Britain spent an average of 3.1 percent of GDP on defense during the last third of the 19th century. One percent of British population was under arms and this is similar to what America spent on its military obligations in the 1990's. In 2001, America spent just 2.9 percent of its budget, which was the lowest level since Pearl Harbor. During the Cold War, spending for the military was substantially higher and yet, the average American income increased. Since the Reagan era, we had essentially seen a two-decade long economic expansion interrupted briefly by two mild recessions. (Recent Bush defense increases will still leave Defense spending as a percent of the GNP significantly lower than during the peak of the cold war.)

The Iraq conflict is an example. The estimated cost of the war is $75 billion but this is a drop in the bucket when compared to a 10.6 trillion dollar economy, which is less than 1 percent of national income. As the economy recovers its steam, the actual war-cost share of GDP will slip to virtually nothing. As economist Larry Kudlow noticed about the 1960's, "Many blamed the battle against the spread of communism in Southeast Asia for the economic woes at home, but the mistaken application of liberal Keynesian fine-tuning was the culprit."

The point is that one can manage significant military overseas missions with a free market, low tax regime. If anything, it would be more difficult to support a worldwide mission with a socialistic state. In the 1980's, Ronald Reagan reinvigorated the American economy with tax cutting policies and soaring military spending. The economy expanded and the Soviet Empire collapsed at the end of the decade. While George Bush leads America in a war against terrorism and the terrorist's protectors, bad economy policy can undermine Bush's mission. Keep tax rates low, regulatory costs minimized and stabilized money and America can repeat the British accomplishment of maintaining peace abroad and prosperity.

3

Changes For The Future

The upcoming decade will be violent as a new world is rising from the ashes of the old. After the end of the cold war, the United States was the lone world power but underneath the surface during the roaring 90's—there was violent counter-revolution brewing. In his book, "Fighting for the Future" Ralph Peters views history as the study of war and documents a generation of new warriors whose major goal is chaos and anarchy. Many developing countries are fragile and as Mr. Peters notes, "it does not take many enthusiastic killers to trigger the destruction of a fragile society." Peters observed that the Bible is "drenched in violence and its moral tenets arose in the response to a violent world. In book after book, we encounter massacre, genocide, ethnic cleansing, rape, plunder, kidnapping, assassination, ineradicable hatreds, and endless warfare."

We began the 90's with a debate between whether we are in the beginning of a new conflict between civilizations or at the end of history. I believe that the answer is both. We are now in the midst of a battle between civilizations. Many in the Islamic world are now rising in revolt against the West and Western values. As Ralph Peters mentioned in his book, "Humans are threatened by change, and in a world in which Western values dominate, there are many who fear the New World. Humans do not want change, they want their custom validated. They want more material possessions, but they do not want to alter their accustomed patterns of behavior to get these things." What we are witnessing is the collapse of government and anarchy being spread by various terrorist organizations as a reaction to the changes that are occurring within their culture.

From the Sudan throughout the Middle East, criminals and warlords are running governments. Tribal and family allegiances are more important than allegiances to the Nation-state that we know today. Many Western diplomats have designed policy that fails to realize the power of collective hatred. Many diplomats believe that we have reached the end of history, while whole groups of people who do not accept the West as their model, and who have virtually declared war on Western values. Western culture dominated by Anglo-Saxon factions is reshaping the earth. Throughout the world, our culture is spread through international corporations, movies and television. Many third world nations appreciate, fear and even hate what they see and sometimes all three emotions are present. Mass media is now the single leading cause of cultural disorientation as our culture competes with home cultures throughout the world. Envy of our values is becoming the norm. The first key to success in this New World is to accept that there are people who hate us and who will not negotiate. Large areas of the developing nations have found none of the progress they imagined after colonialism ceased to exist. Because of petty dictators, kleptomaniacs and socialist dreamers, many of the developing nations fail to produce basic goods for their people. Sub-Saharan Africa is evolving into a band of warlords and tribal leaders as government disintegrates. Starvation and mass genocide has been the rule for the past decade in much of Sub-Saharan Africa, and in the Middle East nationalism and fundamentalism has combined to create a chaotic condition that threatens to engulf the whole world.

The 21st century will be one of constant conflicts, as conflicts will multiply throughout the world. There is a counterrevolution against the rise of Western values and Democratic institutions. As America continues to dominate economically, she will become wealthier, more powerful and a threat to local cultures. We will thus encounter more hatred. We are entering a period of cultural clashes as Western ideals extend throughout the world. Before the end of history and the victory of western ideals, we must battle other cultures alien to our own. Such clashes will be bloody and not conducted by the rules of the Geneva Convention. For peace and our vision of a just society to succeed, we will have to win a major war against the new forces of terror. The End of history can only be accomplished when we win the war on terrorism.

Kenichi Ohmae in his book, "The End of Nation-States," speaks of a world in which nation boundaries matter less as various economic pockets will strike across Nation-states boundaries. Mr. Ohmae's thesis begins with the malleable nature of capital. Capital can move across nation's boundary with the flick of a computer key. Regional economic centers throughout the world are undermining nation-states as natural business units have risen to satisfy the welfare of citizens and improve the quality of life around the globe. For example, economic region states such as Tijuana and San Diego, the Silicon Valley and the Bay Area as well as Hong Kong with adjacent portions of China have formed across national boundaries. If a country's economic policy is not acceptable to investors, then capital will flow elsewhere where economic returns are better. Mr. Ohmae's theory is based on the end of History, but Ralph Peters has the opposite theory on the fate of Nation-states, especially in the third world. In Mr. Peters' neighborhood, various terrorist organizations working with specific outlaw nations are undermining many of the states they reside in. When the Taliban and Al Qaeda controlled Afghanistan, Afghanistan resembled more a mafia operation than a real nation. In Somalia and other African nations, warlords rule over various sections of each nation, and there is no central government to speak of.

As I stated, I believe in the end of history as the eventual acceptance that Western values are now taking hold worldwide. Before Western values become universal, then conflict between cultures will ensue. This does not mean that we are going to be involved in a perpetual war of civilization but we must recognize that many throughout the world will rebel against the principles of freedom and economic progress as represented by the United States.

4

Looking Forward

Michael Leeden stated in his book, "The War Against The Terror Masters" that the "longer we wait the more difficult our tasks will be, and the higher the price we will have to pay." Leeden's theory is that we must convince many outside our circle, in particular the Islamic world, that their best path is to cooperate with the civilized world and that the "Terror Masters have misled their followers and brought nothing but terror and poverty." For Leeden, we have the opportunity this time to bring the Islamic world out of its medieval thought processes and into the 21st century.

The United States has the opportunity to change the face of the Middle East. Leeden has been an observer of Iranian politics and now finds the time is right to end the rule of the Mullahs. Everyday, the common Iranian citizen rebels against their fundamentalist rulers after two decades of economic deprivation. The Iranian mullahs are now ready to join the Nazi movement and the Soviet Empire in the ash heap of history. The new technology of the Internet is allowing the average Iranian to see what they are missing, and they are becoming less tolerant of the present regime.

The present Iranian government has supported terrorist organizations such as Hamas and Hizbullah and even the "moderates" in the present government have as their goal to remove the United States in the Middle East. Even under the Shah, Iran dreamed of being a dominant Regional power—only under the Shah, there was a formal alliance with the United States.

Now with the collapse of Saddam's Iraq; the domino could push Iran's fundamentalist regime into the ash heap of history. Like in Iraq, there is an educated middle class that can pick up the pieces. This is easier to accomplish since before the rise of power of the Iranian fundamentalists, Iran was an American ally in the Region. Iran could easily be part of a western orbit again after the collapse of the mullahs and this will have repercussions throughout the Region. What happens in Iran will not only affect the Middle East but will have an enormous effect on what happens in Afghanistan and maybe beyond. Right now the Iranians are attempting to undermine the embryonic Afghan government, but a western oriented Iran could add stability to Afghanistan, and a Western oriented Iraq will end OPEC as a cartel.

Saddam's Iraq, the opposite side of the coin from Iran, was a secular totalitarian state based on Arab Nationalism as opposed to Islamic fundamentalism, but the objective was the same—the removal of a United States presence from the Middle East. As long as the United States remained the lone superpower and is involved in the Middle East, neither Iraq nor Iran could step forward to dominate the Middle East. The Iraq-Iran War was a war to see who would be the Regional superpower in the Middle East, but the war proved inconclusive. The first Gulf War ended Saddam as a leading military power in the Region, and the second Gulf War permanently assigned his regime to the ash heap of history. The presence of the United States has restrained Iran from extending her power as well.

Saddam's removal was the first linchpin to American policy in the Middle East. Eliminate Saddam, and you set in motion a chain of events that will restructure the entire Middle East. Saddam, whose megalomaniac visions have led to disaster, saw himself as the new Saladin leading the Arab world in battle against the West. Saddam underestimated American resolve before the Gulf War and when President George Bush began the second Gulf war, Saddam's regime end was guaranteed.

The recent Palestinian-Israeli conflict is a sideshow, but many of the major players in the Middle East are using the Palestinians as cannon fodder for their own interests. Iranian support for terrorist groups such as Hizbullah and Hamas has been instrumental in expanding the conflict. One of the goals was to tie the United States down in "the peace process," and it would have delayed or hopefully postponed indefinitely the Iraqi campaign. It did not work. The original game plan was that as long as Palestinians died, maybe Iraqi Republican Guards would not. This strategy failed.

It could have been argued that Iraq did not pose a significant threat to our interests in the Middle East but Saddam's pursuit of a nuclear weapon could have threatened the balance of power in the region. If the Israelis did not bomb the

Iraqi nuclear plant in 1981, neither Gulf War may have happened, and radical Islamic and Arab nationalists would dominate the Middle East today.

Iraq is not a fertile ground for the radical Islamic message of its neighbors, and like Iran, there are significant educated elites that could emerge in a budding democratic state. Iraq itself is a conglomerate state composed of Sunni Arabs, Shiite Arabs, and Sunni Kurds. Kurds have been looking for their own homeland, and in the past, some experts have called for creation of a Kurdish state in Northern Iraq. The rub here is that Turkey would never allow a Kurdish state in its own backyard out of fear that such a state would have claim on its own land.

Other experts visualize "an autonomous Kurdish state within a federated Iraq", leaving open the question, could a federation Iraq work? The Old Ottoman Empire gave minorities substantial autonomy and this helped preserve the Empire for over 400 years. After the fall of the Empire, many minorities became victims of the various new nation-states that rose in the place of the Turkish Empire. The Kurds have been fighting the Iraqis as well as their own neighbors. The interesting aspect is that under American protection the Kurds are slowly developing a nation within a nation, and Post—Saddam Iraq would have to give the Kurds significant autonomy.

Post Saddam Iraq needs to develop a decentralized government giving—Kurds and Shiites—a significant voice both politically and economically. Too often in the Third World, centralized governments deny basic freedoms of expression and security of property even to their ethnic and religious majorities. An Iraq reconstituted as a federated republic with considerable autonomy for the provinces, a demilitarized central government and an even handed and consistent civil law, could provide something new for its devastated peoples: peace and prosperity.

Once we begin the process of integrating the Middle East into the mainstream of the world polity, we will see a major reduction of terrorist activities worldwide. Without active support of sponsor states, Terrorists can't survive long. No base to strike at the West. Also, the domino effect extends beyond the Middle East. Beyond Afghanistan lies Pakistan, a nuclear-armed Islamic power. For the past half century, Pakistan has been an island of instability threatening India by promoting a jihad into the Indian province of Kashmir—a predominately Muslim state within the borders of India. For many in the Pakistan military there are dreams of extending their leadership into an Islamic state that extends into Afghanistan and includes Kashmir; a super Pakistan Islamic State. Unfortunately for Pakistan, they have neither the military means nor the economic strength to make this vision succeed. In 1971, Pakistan proved incapable of keeping East Pakistan (now Bangladesh) and now has a stronger and bigger Hindu State, India to its south that will never allow a greater Pakistan to exist.

Pakistan is tied through its connection to the British Empire, and American aid has helped keep the country afloat. Many Pakistanis just want to have a better life and for years, they have shown their willingness to elect more moderate Islamic leaders as opposed to hardcore fundamentalists. During the 1980's the Pakistani leadership tolerated fundamentalists within its midst, but now Pakistan's present leader, President Musharraf is trapped. He has to deal with many fundamentalists that exist as a threat to his leadership while having at the same time to deal with India. The war on terror has forced Pakistan to decide on which side they belong. For the past decade, Pakistan has played a double game, helping the Taliban keep power in Afghanistan, possibly aiding North Korea with its nuclear plan while obtaining missile technology to strike at India. This was being done, while proclaiming their support for our position. Even today, Pakistan's leadership is attempting to keep playing the double game, but it is more dangerous since the wrong choice could lead to a military disaster. India is running out of patience in dealing with Islamic terror in Kashmir and within India proper. We have allowed President Musharraf leeway in dealing with the Islamic fundamentalists within his midst, but soon India's patience will run out.

Scholar Brink Lindsey views today's acts of terrorism as a return of the barbaric invaders from the Steppes in ancient times. Mr. Lindsey recently wrote that we "find ourselves, once more, in that paradoxical vulnerability that our forebears suffered for more than 20 centuries. The old menace, long vanquished, has returned in new guise. An enemy whose weaknesses in peace become strengths in war threatens us again. Our civilization is exposed to ruin by the very sources of its greatness. After a long respite, the barbarians are at the gate again."

As Mr. Lindsey reminds us, barbaric leaders such as Attila the Hun, Genghis Khan, and Tamerlane arrived from the steppe and delivered catastrophic and even fatal blows to one great civilization after another. The Huns ended Rome as an Empire and the Chinese struggles against the Mongols may have prematurely ended a Chinese industrial revolution causing the Chinese to look inward and atrophy as a civilization. As Western civilization surged to world dominance, the barbarians' invasion that so plagued past civilizations was now a mere memory—words on a page in a history book.

September 11, 2001, changed that once again and now the Barbarians are back at the gate. With over 3,000 innocent American and foreign nationals killed, we found ourselves at war with a new group of terrorists, the new Barbarians. Like past Barbarians, they were not interested in building a new civilization—just destroying the old that is in front of them. They war with their own as they do with us. The shadow now is over us all. The secret of our success is as Brink Lindsey writes, "The West is rich because its people participate in a globe-spanning, mind-boggling complex division of labor. Every moment of our lives is supported and enhanced by the anonymous creativity and hard work of untold millions of people."

Lindsey, like Leeden and others sees this past barbarian threat growing "out of civilizational backwardness." Specifically, the Islamic radicals who now plot against us are a product of the political, economic, and cultural failures of the underdeveloped world. Brooding resentment of those failures has mixed with fundamentalist Islam to produce a totalitarian ideology bent on an apocalyptic showdown with the West." What is needed is a renewed confidence in our institutions and ourselves. Many countries of the third world are filled with corrupt officials and inadequate courts with irrational laws that force the populace to exist in a black market economy. In contrast, we have built a civilization that is based on the rule of law, economic and political freedom. That is now being threatened. The original nomads' invasion ended when their geographical base was eliminated. Thus underpinning the theory of Michael Leeden's ideas that to deal with our present barbarian adversaries, we must rob them of their sponsor states.

To win this war, we must now accept one central truth. *Our civilization and culture, in all of its imperfection, is superior to our barbarian adversaries. We must act on that conviction.* We can no longer accept that civilizations or cultures are no different from another. They are not. Whether it is debating in the UN or in various world forums, no more apologies for our freedom and wealth. We do not need lectures from the likes of Syria or China about human rights or cultural imperialism. Maybe a little Western cultural imperialism might not be so bad.

This process also means that we must be prepared to act to defend our interests and bring the world along. If Europe fears an American hegemony over a barbarian assault upon their own culture, then it is our duty to convince them otherwise. It is not okay for North Korea to have the bomb and blackmail us for assistance while threatening the stability of both South Korea and Japan. It is not okay for Islamic terrorists to kill us with impunity without a price being paid.

The new war on terrorism is merely a repeat of history as new Barbarians appear upon the horizon to threaten civil order and progress. They are not interested in building but destruction. We have an obligation to future generations to defend what we have and prevail.

5

English—World Wide Language

English is the language of the world and it is through language that the Empire of Liberty will be spread. Indian writer, Gurcharan Das, wrote, "English has become the global language at a time when technological breakthrough has shrunk the world." Mr. Das observed that his grandfather treasured his knowledge of the English language as his greatest possession for English united the Indians intelligentsia and civil servants. (The present Indian Constitution recognizes 14 languages as official languages so English is a unifying language in a nation with various sectional dialects.) Mr. Das said the English language, "introduced Indian minds to liberal ideas and the ideals of the French Revolution, while the British Empire was practicing the opposite through colonial rule. Schools and colleges taught liberty and equality while the rulers practiced subjugation and inequality."

English became India's portal to Western thoughts, and Mahatma Gandhi used the British rule of law against the English in his quest to liberate India. The English taught the Indians the language of Liberty, and Indians demanded what was rightly theirs—in English. Within a couple of generations, English may be the dominant language of India, and most likely by the end of this decade, India will be the world's largest English speaking nation. The English language contains nearly a half-million words, which is nearly fivefold more than French, and is constantly changing and growing as its reach expands beyond England and North America.

Scholar Brad DeLong speculates that the Internet will expand international trade and many of these jobs created will be white-collar jobs. Those who speak English will be the major benefactors of this movement and this will encourage English to stay as the world major language of communication. Economist Arnold Kling in a recent piece wrote, "In the era of the English dominated Internet, to speak another language is to impose a barrier on the fastest-growing component of international trade." In Israel, there was a debate on whether to teach high-level technical courses in English or in Hebrew nearly 50 years ago. It was decided to teach these courses in Hebrew but today many Israelis maintain their web presence in English to reach a wider audience beyond Israel.

Some disagree with the theory that English will continue as the dominant language. Nicholas Negroponte of MIT Media Lab believes that Chinese will be the dominant language within a decade and "English speakers will find themselves on the wrong end of the digital divide." Negroponte adds, "We're going to see again, a real rise in multilingual systems and of course multilingual, in my opinion."

Kling disagrees for now, "the Internet revolution is boosting the economic prospects of the English speakers of the world. This includes the countries where English is primarily spoken, as well as the people in other countries who happen to be educated in English."

I agree with the Kling theory for the simple reason that American economic and military preponderance throughout the world allows English to stay dominant. English first was spread worldwide through the British Empire, which extended the language throughout Asia, the Middle East and Africa. From Hong Kong to Africa, the British Empire was home to nearly a quarter of the world population in the 19th century and this allowed English to become the worldwide language, and the emergence of America in the 20th century merely cemented it. As long as America is the leading military and economic power, then English will still be the dominant language. With the emergence of India as a potential superpower and the rise of Indian information technology challenging the United States, English will continue to be the prevailing language in the 21st century. Bangalore in India is the Silicon Valley of Southern Asia and who knows, India may yet supplant America as the new economic power in this new century.

English is the dominant language throughout the world coming as the result of the spread of the British Empire in the 19th century and the emergence of the United States in the second half of the 20th century. The result is that western ideals have been spread throughout the world and this has enabled our values to triumph. With India soon becoming the leading English-speaking nation, these values will no longer be a western value but a worldwide value. There will no longer be an East or West but democratic values that are universal complemented by the language of liberty—English.

By becoming the world's language, English is moving the Anglo culture throughout the world. The United States is part of a broader coalition that is slowly evolving. Scholar and writer James Bennett terms this coalition as "Anglosphere." Mr. Bennett writes, "To be part of the Anglosphere requires adherence to the fundamental customs and values that form the core of English-speaking cultures. These include individualism, rule of law, honoring contracts and covenants, and the elevation of freedom to the first rank of political and cultural values." Bennett observes that these nations share a historical story, which includes the Magna Carta, the American Constitution and the Bill of Rights. Knowing English does not make a person a part of the Anglosphere, but knowing the language shapes the person in those values of the Anglo cultures.

Who is part of the Anglosphere? Good Question and James Bennett answers," Geographically, the densest nodes of the Anglosphere are found in the United States and Great Britain, while Anglosphere regions of Canada, Australia, New Zealand, Ireland, and South Africa are powerful and populous outliers. The educated English-speaking populations of the Caribbean, Oceania, Africa and India constitute the Anglosphere's frontiers."

Ramesh Ponnuru calls this alliance "The Empire of Freedom" which he says is where the United States belongs. Anglosphere may be a branch of Western Civilization that is moving beyond the West and on its own as Ponnuru writes, Anglosphere is "no longer purely Western civilization." Bennett writes that the Anglosphere is "Western in origin but no longer entirely Western in composition and nature, this civilization is marked by a particularly strong civil society, which is the source of its long record of successful constitutional government and economic prosperity." While Europeans are attempting to build a European Union that is bureaucratic in nature, the Anglospheres are for the most part suspicious of such Superstate institutions built from the top down, and instead as Bennett states, "promote more and stronger cooperative institutions, not to build some English-speaking Superstate on the model of the European Union, or to annex Britain, Canada or Australia to the United States but rather to protect the English speaking nations' common values from external and internal fantasies."

What we may be witnessing is a cooperative alliance based on defense alliances and trade. Ponnuru notes, "important point here is that all three countries remain broadly in harmony on the subject of global free trade, and more supportive of free trade than most countries outside Anglosphere."

Of course, Anglosphere may be just another word for American led Empire of Liberty. While some feel that Europe is going in one direction and the United States and other Anglosphere nations another direction, Ponnuru notes, "Is it inconceivable that the political cultures of France and Germany could change into a free-market and pro-American direction in 20 years—or even ten?" As Ponnuru observed, Ireland is becoming an economic dynamo based on free market ideals, so Europe is not yet lost. While the European experience is different from North America, there is still enough similarity between the two separate cultures.

John O' Sullivan has called for an American policy that is pro-American while undermining the Superstate structure of European Union. With many central European countries allying themselves with America, France's leadership in Europe is threatened. While the present German government has joined France in attempting to move forward the Super European Superstate, there is no guarantee that the gambit will succeed. Germany needs to tie Central Europe to modern Europe, and many Central Europeans want an American presence in Europe to safeguard their security. So Germany has to accept an American presence as a price for the expansion of the EU.

English is the language of the Anglosphere and this language helped to assimilate past immigrants and as Bennett states, "Today's Anglospherists see immigrants forming a new layer of intra-Anglosphere ties, as the East and South Asian, Caribbean, and Mediterranean origins of immigrants throughout the Anglosphere create new cross-relationships."

The power of the English language is under girded by the spread of Anglo-Saxon values but this value is worldwide. As I mentioned previously, the presence of Anglosphere is no longer a Western phenomena but a worldwide phenomena. Where the English language permeates, American/British values travel with it. India, North America, The British Isles and Australia are part of a unique cultural trend that stretches throughout the world.

6

Europe at the Crossroads

The current foreign policy of Germany's Gerhard Schroeder and France's Chirac is to push Europe in a new direction under the guidance of a unified French-German leadership. It appears that either Germany or France—or in some cases, both—produced policies guaranteed to irritate the United States. While Rumsfeld dismisses it as the mutterings of the "Old Europe", there are some fundamental changes going on within the European landscape. For the past half century, the United States State Department encouraged a de facto United Europe, integrated economically and politically.

Now many within the European intelligentsia see this as an opportunity to place this United Europe as a rival to the United States to check American hegemony. France and Germany, in particular, want to shape Europe in their image, bureaucratic and socialist to protect their own economic policies and keep the subsidies flowing to their constituents. Throwing out the idea of a joint presidency of the European Union to be manned by German and French leaders as well as a plan for joint Franco-German citizenship, the goal of the German and French intelligentsia is a step toward a possible Franco-German federal union.

These moves are a power move to tell the rest of Europe from the English Channel to the Russian borders that a permanent Franco-German bloc will control Europe's destiny. This modern day Leviathan is rushing fast to gain control since the European Union is enlarging and the new nations may not prove to be ameliorable to a Europe controlled by a Franco-German bloc. Throughout Europe there is a surge of Anti-American feeling over the recent Gulf War, and by destroying the European consensus over American policy of Iraq, the French and German are playing a high stakes game by challenging America's role in NATO. It is time for America to redesign her policy toward the Europeans.

Gulf War II demonstrated a divide within Europe and for the first time, all of Europe is now seriously debating its future and whether they really want a Franco-German leadership. Even within Germany, the debate is not yet settled. Schroeder barely won his last election and in many off elections since then, his party has been devastated. There are Germans who see the folly of Schroeder's vision and the economic downturn has created a new opportunity for Schroeder's opponents. The next German general election could bring a leader friendlier to American interests. As for the French, Chirac is riding high for his anti-American behavior. The French intelligentsia has always demonstrated anti-American feelings but such immature behavior was tolerated during the cold war since France had no inclination to undermine American efforts toward the Soviet Empire. Even De Gaulle understood the difference between the Soviet Empire and America. With the demise of the Cold War, France no longer has to consider a larger Geopolitical reality. For France, her glory rests in a Franco-German leadership over Europe with the French riding the horse.

For Eastern Europeans, a Europe neither allied or actually led by the United States will be its own nightmare. With the Russians to the East and resurgent Germans to the West, Eastern Europeans are not about to trust their security to the Germans or the French. For Eastern Europe, there is history of their sovereignty being sacrificed by the Greater European powers. Their freedom came as the result of American power and idealism. Conservative forces in Italy, Spain, Denmark and even Germany as well as those of Eastern Europeans are clearly allied with America for a less rigid European Union, and acceptance of American leadership as a counterbalance to the European left that dominates the political landscape of Germany and France.

While it is tempting to call Germany and France the old Europe, and it is true that Europe as a continent is several hundred years in the making-it is also true that Europe as a functioning Democracy is younger than the United States and Great Britain. And for most of the past half century, Western Europe has been relieved of its defense responsibility by the United States, so there is a lack of maturity that exists within the defense and intelligentsia of these countries. Now Europe has to play a greater role in world affairs and what passes for policy is nothing more than political pap. Policies based on dreams are not functioning policies. Diplomacy has to be backed up by military power and Europe has been unwilling to spend on military power. As the crisis in the Balkans demonstrated in the 90's, it was American military might that determined the final result.

Many European leaders have learned the wrong lessons of the past fifty years. At this moment, Europe is at peace and for the first time in a millennium, there exists no prospect of a major European war. With the implosion of the Soviet Empire, the subsiding of the Balkan crisis and Russia turning westward, Europe lives in peace. This peace came as a result of American steadfast military support of Western Europe, and now Europe is being integrated through diplomacy. Most European diplomats find that the peace obtained through negotiations can work anywhere. What is missing from the European mindset is the reality that outside Europe, there exists the law of the jungle. After the end of the Gulf War, the American Secretary of State must deal with the Middle East, North Korea, and the possibility of a nuclear crisis in Southern Asia between India and Pakistan. European diplomats will consider Europe their main sphere of interest. There is a different worldview between a European diplomat and an American diplomat. A century ago, it would be the European diplomat that took a worldview and the American diplomat who would consider their backyard as their priority. That has changed. Europe's ability to project military power beyond Europe proper pales in comparison to America's ability in the same arena.

So what should American policy be? It is now time to form alliances with pro-American members including many in the Eastern European corridor and time to rethink the need for a European rapid reaction force. German and French counter moves will be able to offer Eastern Europeans market access and subsidies to frustrate American influence. What will be required is one bold move; drown Europe in an ocean of Atlanticism. The one goal is to push our values and interest to all of Europe. Prime Minister Tony Blair of Britain has been trying to integrate the British isle into Europe. Maybe it is time for Blair to argue our case to Europe as part of the Anglo-Saxon counterweight.

The United States could begin with a transatlantic free trade area that includes Turkey and is open to all European countries and Russia. Many including Steve Forbes and columnist John O' Sullivan have proposed this idea. After the war, NATO must be reconfigured as an American led alliance since the Europeans cannot fund both an independent force and NATO. NATO troops presently in Germany could be moved to Central Europe. NATO troop presence in Central Europe will provide a direct link of American commitment to Europe in the area it will be felt most—the newly freed countries of the former Soviet Empire.

The free trade zone will prove a counterweight to the socialistic super state being created by France and Germany. For Great Britain, cementing the special relations will provide it with a safety valve, entrance into NAFTA and permanent access to American markets. Great Britain will not need Europe but maybe Europe will need Britain. Right now the Franco-German forces have the upper hand but this can change. As mentioned previously, Germany can easily be one election away from changing its own apparent anti-American policy. As for France, this is Chirac's final shot at glory and while he has the upper hand over his domestic foes, this could easily back fire. His disastrous intervention in the Ivory Coast region, and the aftermath of the Gulf War could prove the folly of France's break with America, as France may find itself isolated in Europe. The goal of any American policy should be continued American involvement in Europe. While France may find it bothersome, many in Eastern Europe will find it necessary for their long-term interest.

While this would overturn an American policy of a half-century, it is now time to change our policy toward Europe. The United States allowed Europe a hand in determining our policy in the past decade and what we have seen is a combination of leftist anti-American rhetoric combined with a lack of appreciation of our aid in its own past history.

The UN has failed it biggest test in the past decade as it proved irrelevant in dealing with Saddam Hussein. The UN is an anachronistic relic whose existence gives second and third tier powers the idea that they are important to world events. Let's face it, an organization that allows Libya to head its human rights commission and had Saddam's Iraq scheduled to head its disarmament commission to be followed by Iran is hard to take seriously. One nation is guilty of violating every UN disarmament resolution over the last decade and the other is in the process of building a nuclear weapon. (Of course, Saddam learned about America's version of disarmament the hard way.)

When Yugoslavia was disintegrating in the 90's, the Europeans and the UN made demands on the Serbs, but when push came to shove, the Serbs merely ignored the UN and the Europeans. The Srebrenica safe zone tragedy showed the impotence of the UN. Muslims, whose safety was guaranteed by the UN, were massacred by Serbian troops as Dutch troops did nothing. The UN guaranteed their safety but thousands of Muslim males were butchered. The downside was that these troops were in harms way but had no intention of fighting and dying for someone else. It was for show and when the bluff was called, the innocent were killed. It was not until the United States got involved militarily without UN approval that peace came to the Balkans.

The United Nations will not be a serious instrument in preventing future wars and no future UN resolution supporting war will be taken seriously. When Hans Blix basically stated in several reports that Iraq was flouting UN directives, there was no real demand to ensure compliance. What the UN called for were increased inspectors as if this was going to do any good.

The reality is that many members of the UN do not follow even the most basic of human rights. So, the idea that the UN will be an instrument of peace when many of its own members are part of the problem is what undermines its legitimacy. Why should Saddam's Iraq even be part of the United Nations or for that matter, Iran, Syria, Libya and other totalitarian states? Having Iraq in the United Nations or Libya at the head of the Human Rights Commission is like having the local Mafia don the chief of police and many of his henchmen members of the police force.

When Iraq was found in violation of 1441, no one disputed it. And many nations were perfectly willing to allow Saddam to stay in power. So why does the UN matter anyway? It doesn't. Not as an agency for peace.

Over the next decade, new alliances and new arrangements will be made. What made the UN work was the willingness of the United States to surrender some of its leverage to its allies within the body and the willingness of the United States to use force to back up its interests. The cold war did not end because of the United Nations but due to American military power.

In the 19th century, general peace was kept in Europe because of a balance of power and for most of the century the great powers assured that balance of power kept a major European war from breaking out. World War I ended a relative era of peace and the 20th century saw two major eruptions. The League of Nations failed to prevent World War II since the major powers that inhabited it used the organization as an excuse not to act as any preventative measure against war. *The United Nations is similar in that respect; it is an organization that allows nations excuses not to act.*

Over the past 50 years, we have had leaders who pretended to pay attention to the United Nations but when push comes to shove, ignored the UN when American interests were at stake. Did Clinton ask UN permission to bomb Kosovo? No. Did JFK, Lyndon Johnson or Richard Nixon ask the UN permission to fight the Vietnam War? No. Rarely have we asked for United Nations permission. The first Korean conflict was a fluke as the Russian UN ambassador was not present for the UN vote, so Russia could not veto U.N. participation in the war. If the UN did not support the United States, Truman would have continued to defend South Korea. The first Bush would have gone to War against Saddam in 1991 if the UN did not cooperate. The UN was merely a cover for primarily an American operation.

For those serious about American foreign policy, the UN will not be a major factor. For Europeans, the UN gives them a say in world affairs and the illusion that what works in Europe will work worldwide. This is a dangerous illusion in a dangerous world. For the serious, the UN is nothing but a distraction that allows the enemies of freedom to stall. For the idealist, the UN represents the last best hope of humanity. The realists are right and the idealist is wrong.

The future of NATO will differ markedly from its past. The Soviet Empire is over but new threats are occurring. NATO has expanded but it will play a support role to the United States. During the Kosovo air war, the United States flew two-thirds of the strike missions and nearly the entire high tech precision-guided missile supply came from the United States. European air forces were limited due to a lack of computerized weapons, night vision equipment and advanced communications.

NATO needs to be more flexible. We may be witnessing a two-tiered NATO with coalitions of willing nations cooperating with the United States on selected missions outside of the United States with neither NATO nor the EU having veto power when the United States chooses to act alone.

Ethnic strife/totalitarian order/state managed economies or International cooperation/decentralized power/economic, these are the respective formulae for chaos or freedom. A Pax Americana would be an empire unlike the Roman—based not upon armed occupation but upon the ideals of freedom that are four thousand years old. These ideas hold that prosperity is rooted not in the councils of bureaucrats, but in the minds of free men created by a Supreme Being. The United States as the remaining power can help to shape this world not just materially but metaphysically and morally. What this requires, simply is that we have as much faith in our fundamental institutions as those outside our borders seem to have.

7

Russia, China, and Europe

After 9/11 is humankind headed toward peace and prosperity, based on economic liberty? Or are we entering a period of fragmentation, marked by wars of race and religion? I posed this question a few years back to a number of individuals widely known for their writings on global politics. In 1990, with the breakdown of totalitarian governments, human expectations were raised to their highest pitch. From Warsaw to Managua and from Peking to Lima, people felt the breath of change and the hope of freedom.

In China, the search for the "new man" in the image of Mao is over. In China, the revolution from below is continuing; many of the economic reforms of the past decade are being expanded. Chinese Society is rife with crosscurrents and Chinese pragmatism is instituting economic freedom piecemeal. The communist bureaucracy is struggling to retain centralized control of the political process. But as people gain economic freedom, they will eventually demand political freedom as well. Of course, the danger remains the reverse could occur—Hong Kong, long a haven of capital formation and enterprise, threatens the hegemony of the Communist authority. In the territory adjacent to Hong Kong, economic enterprise is spilling over and this may yet spread throughout China proper.

Taiwan is still a reminder to the Mainland of a different way. Taiwan has always been economically ahead of China proper in developing the economic good to the common people, and the goal of uniting Taiwan to China represents two objectives. The first is that it brings more access to enterprising Chinese under China's control. The other is that as China strives to be the Regional power, shipping lanes in much of the Western Pacific can be controlled by China domination of Taiwan. Taiwan is like an aircraft that would allow China to reach out and influence the Western Pacific arena. As for the average Chinese, the adoption of free market reforms may have gone on too long to be reversed.

China has the potential to be a constructive member of Asia but it could be a fearsome, aggressive and militaristic power. How China handles its differences with Taiwan will be the true bellwether of China's role in the world. Some experts have suggested it would be prudent to integrate Taiwan in the Asia—Pacific economic community as a response to China's aggressive behavior. China wants Taiwan as part of a greater China and there is evidence to show China may yet attempt to use military might to bring Taiwan into the fold.

With Taiwan's deeper economic integration into the Asia—Pacific and international trading community, the less influence China will have on Taiwan's trading partners making it less likely that China can isolate Taiwan. China can be a force for good and stability or it can descend the Pacific Rim into chaotic disarray.

When communism fell in the Soviet Union, there remained a strong desire for the return of democracy among many Russians. Seventy years of central economic planning, secret police, and excessive spending on the military conspicuously failed to make a nation of the Soviet Union. Through the Baltic States of Estonia, Latvia, Georgia, and Lithuania, the Ukraine and in Russia itself, the nationalist movements called for the dismemberment of the central authority: the Communist Party. Here more clearly than anywhere else we can observe the crosscurrents of the totalitarian world. When the Soviets attempted to decentralize economically, the government became decentralized and in the process, the empire was sacrificed. Today, Putin is continuing the reforms of the early 90's and his tax reforms are showing results. Russia is now reasserting itself as a great power as Putin allies himself with Bush in the war on terror. This is allowing Putin to strengthen Russia in the Islamic areas of the former Soviet Empire, and with the apparent collapse of OPEC, Russia stands to prosper with its own energy resources.

Russia's track record since September 11th has been mixed. While Russia has cooperated with the United States in Afghanistan and other aspects of the war on terror, it tried to delay the war on Iraq and still has relations with Iran—even helping Iran with its nuclear program that could result in Iran becoming a nuclear power. Russia's tacit support of Iraq and Iran is due more to profiting from oil and gas deals and an attempt to recover Soviet era debt from these nations. The one area that Russia has been cooperative in is allowing the United States to abrogate the ABM treaty. This gave the United States the green light to develop a strategic defense against ballistic missiles and help possibly cement a future Pax Americana while checkmating any future rogue state from attempting to blackmail the developed nations.

Both China and Russia will challenge American leadership but in different ways. Russia wants to be linked to the West through economic reform but Russia will insist on being an equal partner making it clear to America that it will pursue its own interests. Russia's recent alliance with Chirac's France is just one example that Russia will follow her own interests and not necessarily form a special relationship with the United States. China is already pursuing its own interests but there are areas in which both the United States and China's interests coincide. With the rise of Islamic fundamentalism, China has its own interests to protect as a portion of Western China is impacted. China is not too pleased to have a nuclear North Korea that it can't control at its border. A nuclear-armed North Korea and United States withdrawal from South Korea could mean a nuclear-armed Japan, and even Taiwan may choose to develop its own nuclear capacity. This threatens China's military Regional power.

The European Union is now trying to redefine Europe. As I have stated, France and Germany would love to see a bureaucratically dominated economic policy from Warsaw to London. Others such as Great Britain would love to see more flexibility in economic planning. The EU is attempting to "harmonize" economic conditions throughout Europe, but the French and Germans are attempting to raise government regulations and taxes throughout the continent so they will be the economic leaders. Right now both France and Germany are falling behind their European neighbors and many German business leaders are moving their businesses overseas due to German tax and regulation policies that hinder local economic opportunities. The results are that many jobs and businesses are escaping to areas where friendly tax treatment exists. Capital is moving away from Berlin and Paris elsewhere, thus forcing the French and Germans to begin dismantling a portion of their welfare state or be left behind.

Europe can play a role in cementing Russia's role in the European community. Europe, like the United States, needs to vary their energy needs and one area is Russia. Europe can expand its exports from Russia while opening its market to Russian agricultural products. As Russian agriculture continues on the path of reform, more products will become available for exports, and besides the competition will be good for European consumers. If both Europe and the United States assist Russia's entry into WTO, this will enhance Russia's economic prospect leading to a more stable and friendly Russia. Of course, Europe becoming dependent upon Russian energy could also allow Russia to dictate policy in Europe that will not necessarily be to our benefit.

Capitalism and free trade are the carrot of free world politics. The civil institutions of capitalism—private property rights and civil liberties—underpin the material wealth that is the envy of nations. Armed might and the willingness to use it is the stick, the ultimate disincentive to totalitarians. The debate within Europe is how independent can Europe be of the United States and yet, the gathering storms throughout the world are forcing Europe to ally itself to American interests. The French desire to spread their version of economic theory is undermined by competition on the European continent and with America. Nor will Germany or France in Europe and Japan in the West take over America's role in the world. These countries have economic problems currently, and their own past prevents them from taking military action easily.

The World is not crumbling but changing. The enveloping chaos is the turbulence of people wakening from decades—or centuries—of totalitarian slumber. The final victory of a Pax Americana would be the widespread acceptance that "western" values are only incidentally western. In China and Russia these values are slowing sinking in and in Europe, there is a serious debate about freedom. The coming war on terror will force these states to decide if they want to follow a new path of freedom and progress or watch the world descend into chaos. There will be no one sitting on the sideline.

8

North Korea—The Asian Axis of Evil

North Korea has been a wild card on the international scene since its soldiers invaded South Korea on June 25, 1950. Succeeding crises included the hijacking of USS Pueblo and the 1983 assassination of the South Korean cabinet members in Burma and most recently, its admission that it has been conducting a major clandestine nuclear weapons development for the past several years.

Time has seemingly stopped in Pyongyang, the world's last outpost of Stalinism. Kim Jong II is the son of Kim II Sung, the tyrannical cult figure whose public adulation cloaks the life of their country from the rest of the world. The communications blackout, which Kim's regime imposes, yields an intelligence vacuum on the plans and, indeed the very composition, of the Pyongyang regime. Kim Jong II and his father rule Korea with an iron fist and the internal workings of their regime remain a complete mystery. There are rumors of food riots but given the efficiency of the North Korean security police, there is no organized opposition to the regime. North Korea appears to be a military force with a state attached.

Like the Stalinist Soviet system, which it closely resembles, North Korea's economy is organized in two discrete sectors, both public. The defense sector is competitive with that of many western nations, producing heavy tanks, submarines and missiles—and now apparently, nuclear weapons. Regrettably, armaments are North Korea's primary export, which is why its production of scud missiles and nuclear warheads would constitute a substantial threat to global stability. Among Pyongyang's major clients are the Baathist regime of Syria, and possibly Islamic Iran. The North Korean defense sector accounts for a full 30 percent of that nation's Gross National Product. (The United States spends roughly 3 percent of its GNP on defense by comparison.)

Predictably, the civilian economy is a basket case, spiraling ever downward in the post-Soviet era. Public "energy conservation" programs lead some economists to opine that factories are being run at half capacity. North Korea has traditionally imported its oil from other communist countries; but now China and Russia often insist on hard currency. Two-thirds of the North Korean economy is handled by a barter system thus denying Korean producers access to the world market. Continuing shortages of fertilizer and fuel hamper agriculture. The government is reportedly advancing a "two meals a day" campaign sparking scattered food riots, which may affect even the military sector. Pyongyang denies the rumors.

Like many former communist states in Eastern Europe, pollution is a pervasive problem. North Korea uses coal for 70 percent of its primary energy—the result of autarkic policies aimed at producing "self-sufficiency" in a nation self-quarantined from the capitalist world trading system.

But as elsewhere in the communist world, policies aimed at "self sufficiency" produced no such thing: merely a parasitic bureaucracy straddling an impoverished peasantry. The hard currency North Korea needs to survive comes largely from North Korean emigrant workers, primarily in Japan, who send their wages to the state for the sake of their captive families.

The North Korean economy is far less sophisticated than that of Iran or Syria, whose economy both overt and covert is far more broadly based. Pyongyang is highly vulnerable to sanctions in two areas:

- prohibitions against the export of wages to North Korea by its emigrant nationals; and

- interference with vital oil imports.

The latter requires the cooperation of China, North Korea's traditional ally along with South Korea. North Korea's nuclear program is designed among other things, to blackmail the West, in particular the United States

The dream of unifying Korea under communism still drives the North Koreans. With an economy in tatters, and a political non-system based on cult like worship, the unification of Korea could be similar to what happens to East Germany when the East was absorbed by West Germany. This is the North Korean nightmare—to be incorporated under the auspices of South Korea. They are aiming for the reverse, a Stalinist state over the entire peninsula.

The real problem and the real solution lay with the South. President-elect Roh in a close election won on the platform to continue the sunshine policy of his predecessor. The policy is a failure but in South Korea, there is a great divide between the Generation that survived the Korean conflict and a younger generation that views the United States as the obstacle to Korean unification. Roh is ignorant of the history of the cold war in which German reunification was successful only under the sponsorship of a strong American military presence and the collapse of the Soviet Empire. It was not through appeasement. Allowing anti-American sentiment to fester and use it as a successful tactic to win a political campaign did not serve the interest of the ruling party's candidate. Even Roh's predecessor argued that a South Korea—U.S. alliance remains vital to Seoul's security and to regional stability in general.

Adam Garfinkle, editor of the National Interest, maintains that we should announce the withdrawal of American troops; thus forcing the other powers in the Region to understand and deal with the North Korean threat themselves. As Garfinkle noticed, "The key Chinese interest is that Korea not be nuclearized because it presupposes a nuclear Japan." And he adds, "South Koreans, having to defend themselves will either see the illusions of their own policy or suffer the consequences of maintaining it. But it's their country and, frankly their potential misfortune no longer matters to us as much as it did during the Cold war." Garfinkle's own theory is based on the premise that "we will be far away with deterrence reasonably intact…China, however, cannot relocate." China would have to face the consequences of a nuclear North Korea and possibility of a nuclear Japan or South Korea or help the United States to contain North Korea and participate in its withering away. While I am not yet ready to follow Mr. Garfinkle in bringing home the troops, his ideas have merit. Of course, Bush could offer China a deal-help us contain North Korea and allow the peninsula to be united under South Korea's aegis, and we withdraw from South Korea. The troops can yet be negotiating tools

The North Korean nuclear program threatens the South more than it threatens the United States, with South Korea unable to be a bystander who can sit out any crisis between the North and the United States. South Korea needs to insist that the North follow all of its international obligations. North Korea is part of the Axis of evil in the world, an unpredictable foe in an uncertain world. No one knows what the North Koreans want or will do in the future but one thing is certain; North Korea as a nuclear power threatens world stability.

9

Africa Reviewed

A few years back, I had the opportunity to interview African economist Dr. George Ayittey, a veteran commentator for various journals and newspapers as diverse as the New York Times, The Ghana Drum and the Wall Street Journal. His book, "Africa Betrayed" presents a myth—shattering view of the myriad problems of his native continent.

No friend of western imperialism or black African tyranny, Ayittey contended that the pre-colonial cultures of the African continent were rich in both social and economic institutions—a past that provides the implicit key to a future African renaissance today.

Africa's abysmal realities belie its amazing potential. Compared to the Asian economic tigers—South Korea, Taiwan, Hong Kong, and Japan—Africa is blessed with an abundance of mineral wealth and a relatively low population density.

Pre-colonial Africa was poised in many respects to follow a development curve similar to that of late-medieval Europe. Authoritarian regimes, such as those of the Fertile Crescent, the Nile, the Indus, and the Yellow River were not part of the African heritage. "Land was abundant," Dr. Ayittey wrote, "and tribes that found themselves subjugated could always move elsewhere." The most successful African empires were loose confederations of vassal states. The Ghanaian Empire lasted for some 900 years. By contrast, the Zulu Empire of Shaka, centralized and authoritarian, lasted a mere ten years. Pre-colonial Africans, members of 2,000 tribes were ill inclined toward the authoritarian systems, which impeded modernity in the great empires of the East and Middle East.

Pre-colonial Africa was rich in nascent free market institutions as well. "The means of production in traditional Africa," says Ayittey, "were privately owned and never owned by the Chief or the King.... Village markets were free and the Chief did not fix prices."

Imagine what Europe would have looked like if the twin bulwarks of the Franks and the Byzantines had not prevented the establishment of a trans-Mediterranean Islamic Empire in the middle Ages. Decentralized Europe, isolated in the backwaters of the great authoritarian civilizations, leapt from feudalism, to commercial empire, to industrial empire and finally to political hegemony.

Africa was less fortunate. Successive waves of slavers—first Islamic, then European-were followed by the colonialists. The abrupt departure of the Europeans resulted in totalitarian states based on the structures they'd left behind—bureaucracies not organic to African institutions, unbounded by popular restraints of any kind.

Post-colonial African leadership looked not to indigenous institutions, but to European models, including Marxism and ultra-nationalism. "Our leaders failed us," Ayittey told me, "It is not racism to say that. We need to distinguish between the African people and their leaders." For almost two generations, the African experience has been characterized by one party dictatorships, unrivalled kleptocracy, and declining economic performance, leaving many nations on the continent worse off than ever before. The color of the oppressor's skin gives scant consolation to those who are starving or dying of AIDS.

Corruption is the hallmark of modern Africa. Leaders shifted billions of dollars to Swiss bank accounts while their people survived on a day-by-day basis. Corruption breeds dependency. Billions of dollars in aid flow into Africa each year and much of it is looted. Many African nations spend between a quarter and one half of their GNP on military machines, whose primary purpose is to protect the leaders from their own people.

But for all the money flowing into Africa even more is flowing out. Annually, 15 billion dollars leaves—far more than the aid, which the continent receives. And as long as African leaders refuse to protect property rights and to erect judicial structures of civil liberty, capital will be neither invested nor reinvested. The authoritarian reality underlying the socialist façade undermines all attempts at reform.

Ayittey saw any future renewal must stem from a rebirth of the decentralized political and economic traditions of the continent. The West can help in minor ways. First, Western nations must demand real reform in exchange for aid. Leaders who reject property rights and civil liberties may benefit from Western aid—their peoples do not. Ayittey believed that Africans need training in the art of democracy, much like the residents of Eastern Europe and the former Soviet Union.

Ultimately, Ayittey maintained Africans must solve their own problems. Aid administered through corrupt centralized governments merely exacerbates the continent's problems, reinforcing regimes that ought to fall. Ayittey took the contrarian view that Africa needs less aid not more. Africans must turn to their pre-colonial roots. According to Dr. Ayittey, societal rebirth required loose-con-federated government, which protects tribal rights; political freedoms; and rees-tablishment of property rights. This plan was indeed presented by Dr. James Africanus Horton in 1868.

Leaders of Africa betrayed their people after the "first liberation" from their colonial powers. Their true liberation will come when, recovering their pre-colonial past, they overthrow those who betrayed them.

10

A Federated Iraq—After the War

In my previous book and writings, I reviewed the possibility that a Post-Saddam Iraq would be a federated state with each ethnic group having a say in the government. Iraq becomes a test case of American diplomacy and patience. My own thought then as now is that any Post Saddam Iraq needs to develop a decentralized government giving Kurd, Shiite and Turkoman a significant voice both politically and economically. Iraq, like most Middle Eastern countries, denied basic freedom of expression and security of property. An Iraq reconstituted as a federal republic with considerable autonomy for the provinces and an even-handed and consistent civil law could provide the Iraqi people peace and prosperity.

A glimpse of the future is being seen in North Iraq in the predominately Kurdish states. After the first Gulf War, the Iraqi government blockaded the North and the first winter saw starvation among many Kurds. Infant and adult mortality increased and even today, the children who were born and survived have an abnormally low growth rate. Today, Kurdistan stands transformed, illustrating that a change in governance alters quality of life and shows that a federated Iraq could possibly work. Iraqi Kurds are turning what was a wasteland into a land of prosperity. After a decade of war, the Kurds are now seeing reductions in infant mortality and more births are being seen. Northern Iraq is the most prosperous section of Iraq. Where there stood a Republican Guard base now stands a supermarket. Kurds can buy Italian designer clothing, imported electronics, and Turkish can goods—all being scanned by infrared scanners at checkout counters.

Over the past decade, the Kurds have scrambled to create a political authority. The two major factions, the Kurdistan Democratic Party (KDP) and the Patriotic Union of Kurdistan (PUK) were evenly divided and the early steps in governing did not go smoothly. The coalition government between the two leading parties unraveled and unofficial civil war occurred. Tension between the two exacerbated when the Iraqi Republican Guard swept into portions of Kurdistan driving the PUK into Iran. The KDP cooperated with the Iraqis. Northern Iraq is essentially divided between the two sides and certainly problems exist within Northern Iraq, but it does demonstrate that federalism could work. Since the end of the civil war between the two factions, life has improved for the Kurds as both parties competed to win the hearts and minds of the people. Both sides compete in building playgrounds or Internet cafés, and Michael Rubin of the American Enterprise Institute observed, "Fears that federalism might lead to separatism are misplaced. Administrative federalism involves only devolution of power to each of Iraq's eighteen provinces, keeping the power of the Kurds, Shites, and the Sunnis in balance and preventing the domination of any minority on a national level. A weak central government would retain power over defense and foreign policy."

Many of the major Iraqi ethnic groups support federalism as a means to keep the country together and protect the rights of each minority. A federalist state would encourage competition between Regions to see who can provide the best services for their constituents. Iraq had the potential to be a successful state for it has natural and human resources. Literacy in the 1980's was 80% and this bodes well for Iraq to be able to take advantage of the new technical age. Prosperity is within reach of the average Iraqi. There is a core of engineers and builders who can reconstruct the new Iraq.

A federated and western oriented Iraq will face severe challenges both within and beyond its borders. Surrounded by predators in a tough neighborhood, Iraq would essentially be unarmed after a conflict with the West. Many of Iraq's neighbors will love to see the new Iraq fail and so western, read—American; presence will be required to maintain power. The major military powers left, Turkey and Iran, have their own threats from a federated Iraq.

Turkey's biggest fear is an independent Kurdish state that could encourage its minority within its border to rebel for its own independent state. Turkey has been a steadfast ally of the United States and NATO. The recent actions by France and Germany to deny Turkey's NATO aid could weaken Turkey's long-term alliance with the West, or at least Europe. The United States will maintain its own alliance with Turkey, independent of Europe and at least the United States has influence over Turkey. The United States must regard Turkey's interests and especially its security interests. A federalized Iraq that is economically prosperous will enhance Turkey's long-term interests. For one, Turkey will have access to vital oil supplies and trade between the two nations will boost Turkey's long-term economic prospects. A federated Iraq will encourage the Iraqi Kurds to stay as part of Iraq and reduce the call for an independent Kurdish state, with that federated state respecting all ethnic groups including the Turkoman who are close ethnically to the Turks.

Iran, however, fears a western oriented federated Iraq for it fears that it is the next target of Washington. Iran could use its influence among some Kurdish Islamic groups to undermine the northern federated state but its ability to impact the Shites in Southern Iraq would be compromised by an American presence on Iraq's Southern border. There is a new generation of Iranians, who no longer fear or love the Islamic revolution, and young Iranians are now looking to the West. A federated democratic Iraq will be a positive example to Iranian reformers.

Kuwait would be happiest since its own security will be secured by an American presence in Iraq. The Saudis have been playing their own game of paying off selected terrorist groups to keep them out of the kingdom while trying to be America's ally. Over the past decade, Saudis have attempted to play off America's past support with an unofficial rapprochement with Iran. In the 1970s, there existed an Iranian-Saudi axis when dealing with oil prices but this manipulation ended with Reagan's election. With the radical Iranian fundamentalists threatening the Saudis on one side and many radical states supported by the Soviets on the other hand, the Saudis needed an American guarantee of their survival.

With the end of the cold war, one of the rationales for the alliance ended. With many radical fundamentalists controlling the education and the economic slow-down in Saudi Arabia a new generation of Saudis who favor the more radical Bin Laden approach as opposed to Western thought has been formed. Reform in Iraq will push the Saudis into accelerating their own reform movement and there are many in the Saudi royal family now ready for reform. With Russia becoming a major player in the oil market, and Iraq now part of the Western orbit OPEC is effectively dead, Saudi ability to control events in the Middle East is crippled.

The Middle East has been a harbor of anti-western radicalism that threatens world stability as Islamic-fascists attempt to lead an entire faith in a jihad against the West. Liberating the Middle East from its past will lead to world stability. Afghanistan was the first step and now Iraq is the second step.

11

New Thinking about Nuclear Non-proliferation

When it came to implementing a nuclear non-proliferation policy that works, Israel demonstrated one method in 1981 when they bombed Iraqis nuclear program out of existence—just eradicate the opponent's nuclear capacity before your enemy has a chance to develop a weapon. The present Gulf War II has as one of its goals, destroying Iraq's ability to develop weapons of mass destruction by destroying what weapons they have and replacing Saddam's regime. The American policy is the beginning of a new concept—not all nations are equal nor should all nations have nuclear weapons. Some nations just cannot be trusted with the bomb.

We can no longer keep the nuclear genie in the bottle. There are some nations in whose hands nuclear weapons may in fact be stabilizing. In the 19th century, Europe was dominated by a concert of leading powers, whose goal was to maintain the peace and European stability after the end of the Napoleonic wars. What is required today is a similar concert of democratic states ranging from Japan, India, Russia as well as NATO powers led by the United States to ensure a new stability. In this new era of terror, stability is dependent upon this new concert acting in harmony. Unfortunately The Gulf War II has strained relations among many of those nations required to maintain stability and not all nations have the same interest in restraining rogue nations from getting nuclear weapons. (France was instrumental in helping Iraq get started on its nuclear program and Russia is presently aiding Iran in its nuclear program. It appears that financial consideration is more important than worldwide security.)

The biggest problem with nuclear non-proliferation is the unrealistic approach that good intentions are enough to ensure enforcement. We already know that Israel has nuclear weapons, even though it is not a publicly acknowledged fact.

Israel's nuclear program is strictly designed to send a message to any potential enemy, that attempting a second Jewish holocaust could mean the elimination of a few million Arabs. In the Middle East, Iran and Iraq have been working for years on extending their own nuclear capacity. Nuclear weapons and the missile technology that carries those weapons is a half-century old, so these weapons are easily within the reach of any country with the will and scientific know how. America needs to accept the fact that some nations will obtain nuclear weapons, regardless of international pressure. There is a difference between a nuclear bomb in the hand of a democratic nation such as India, Great Britain or France and the bomb in the hands of Iranian mullahs or a North Korean madman. Nuclear non-proliferation needs to concentrate upon those rogue nations who threaten the general peace.

What would a new policy on nuclear non-proliferation look like? The first is strictly a military response. In 1981, Israel bombed Iraq's nuclear plant and crippled Saddam's nuclear plans. What would have been the result of the Gulf war a decade later had Israel not succeeded in destroying Saddam's nuclear capacity? The problem with this option is that it means that the United States and its western allies must be prepared to take military actions and there is no guarantee that they will be supported by the world. The recent UN debacle demonstrates that reality. Bush's policy of considering preventative war has struck more fear among our allies than our enemies. Israel was condemned by the world including the United States when she struck at Iraq's nuclear capacity. There are other targets and yet, there is no consensus even in the United States to strike at Iran's and North Korea's nuclear facilities. Japan has already declared that it will preempt any North Korean missile launch but does Japan have the will to follow through on its threat? So, a military strike means that the West, in particular the United States or its allies, must be prepared to go to war or at least exercise the guts to implement military options, if appropriate. The military option is not a viable option if there is no will.

The second option is to replace the totalitarian government in question by other means. We had that opportunity with Iraq in 1991 and left Saddam in place. Then we fought a second war to change the regime. Iran is another country, where underground opposition is being developed as a result of the present Mullah's rule. With economic stagnation, the present Iranian government is attempting to reform its economy, but the ultimate scheme has yet to change-the removal of America from the Middle East. Iran has already made its goal of becoming a nuclear power public and they are receiving help abroad. Only a change of the present government will prevent Iran from becoming a nuclear power. Presently there are opposition forces within Iran but will we support them? Not all change of regime will require direct military means but could be accomplished by supporting indigenous forces.

The final solution is simply the adoption of the Strategic Defense Initiative. The use of technology to checkmate the present missile technology allows the West to maintain its military superiority while giving potential nuclear powers a reason not to proceed with their own program. An Iranian nuclear power could be made obsolete by the time it is up and running and SDI allows the West an insurance policy against any cheaters. The days of depending upon mere pieces of paper for security are over. A missile shield allows the United States to protect its own interests, while providing a more stable nuclear umbrella to protect other nations. The reason that the nuclear club has not gotten even bigger is that America's nuclear umbrella has been extended to potential nuclear powers such as Japan and Germany. There is no need for those countries to become nuclear powers in their own right as long as they are allied with the United States. Finally, a strategic defense protects the United States in a world of changing alliances. SDI allows a sensible policy of containment if that is what is required in the future. SDI also allows for reduction in nuclear weapons since it provides nations an insurance policy against cheating and reduces the utilities of nuclear weapons. The Patriot missile system in this recent Gulf war conflict is already showing the utility of this approach. SDI also allows the West options other than military intervention to stop the wrong nations from getting their hands on the bomb.

When North Korea withdrew from the Nuclear Nonproliferation Treaty (NPT), the absurdity of depending upon a scrap of paper became obvious. Recent attempts by the United States to develop a regional alliance to adopt common strategy to deal with North Korea has failed so far. The two options presently are either military option or appeasement. A workable SDI in place would allow an American President to put a defensive shield in place and allow a policy of containment of North Korea to possibly succeed until the North Korean economy implodes. The most important principle of any future nuclear non-proliferation policy is that nuclear weapons in the hands of rogue states can be destabilizing and nuclear weapons in the hands of more mature and democratic states are stabilizing. Accept that principle and more sane non-nuclear proliferation policy can follow.

12

Lessons of Gulf War II

What are the lessons of Gulf War II? Ralph Peters in his excellent series in the NY Post during the second Gulf War summed up his view when he wrote, "Saddam had a classic 20th-century, industrial-age war plan. But our forces fought a 21st-century, post-industrial war." Peters dismissed the notion that Saddam did not have a plan or that he did not put up much of a fight. Peters states, "Far from technically incompetent, Saddam's plan was right out of Clausewitz. Its models were the lessons of the Russian defeat of Napoleon in 1812 and the Soviet victory over the Germans in the Second World War. The principles were: Delay your enemy, attrit his forces, trade space for time, harass his supply lines and husband your best forces for a mighty counterattack. Wait until the attacker has advanced so far into your country that he reaches a "culminating point" at which point he has lost his momentum and his supply lines are overextended. Then strike. Saddam didn't so much plan the defense of Baghdad as he tried to refight the defense of Moscow."

General Franks observed that Speed kills and Colonel Peters followed this thought by observing, "But the campaign the U.S. military fought cast off the rules of the modern era. We fought the first post-modern war. In the final grudge match between Clausewitz and GI Joe, it was a shutout. And no other military on earth could have done it.... The Russian advisors [to the Iraqi army] fail to grasp the profound changes in our military and the American way of war....They clearly had no sense of battlefield awareness, speed, precision and tactical ferocity of America's 21st century forces."

Indian writer Pramit Pal Chaudhuri wrote in India's Hindustan Times, ", Russia provides the type of weapons needed for mass wars of millions of men, thousands of warplanes and tanks. What New Delhi is looking for today is smart weaponry, stuff that will allow it to attack a terrorist camp with smart missiles or stealth-drop commandos. This is exactly what Russia cannot provide. As it is, even the warplanes it sells now have to get their more advanced avionics and missiles from Israel or France." Many nations will re examine their military strategy and the weapons that go with it. Countries like India are now studying our tactics to adopt for their very own.

Throughout the world, our enemies and even our allies are watching and observing what they witnessed. Peters observed that one lesson many rogue states will take from this, "Don't fight the United States." The North Koreans were taking notes and the Chinese as well as they watched the "effectiveness and efficiency of this campaign." As Peters articulated, "Even our own military is surprised at how things went, you may be certain that the boys in Beijing are following events avidly."

Keegan viewed this as an old fashioned war when he agreed with Frank's assessment, "Speed Kills" when he wrote, "the blitzkrieg effect being achieved simply by speed and efficiency of execution." The speed with which this battle took place was breathtaking. Keegan stated, "The dash from Kuwait to the vicinity of Baghdad was done at a speed unequalled in military history. The convoys, moreover, brought not only ammunition, water and food, but also the tanks, loaded on to transporters, without which there would have been breakdowns…The US Army transport services pride themselves, justifiably, on their ability to deliver necessities on time and over distance."

What will be viewed is the flexibility of the American forces. As the old adage goes, a plan fails to survive the first bullet flying and this was certainly the case. The war began with a strike on Hussein's headquarters in an attempt to cut off the head of the regime and when Turkey failed to allow the 4th Army to break from the North, Franks had to change the game plan.

Franks went on a fast break, combining a lightening strike toward Baghdad with armor forces combined with air support. Meanwhile special ops were operating all over the country in a silent war, and small paratroopers combined with special ops worked with the indigenous Kurdish fighters in the North. In Afghanistan, special ops rode on horseback as the flyboys used the latest technology to target the Taliban. In Iraq, the old and the new combined in a similar synergistic form.

What was seen is that the present day American military can now fight any style of combat. While one Russian observer stated that Americans were cowards depending sorely on technology and did not like to go street to street, this war proved that the Americans, borrowing from their British allies, learned street fighting. They did the dirty work while losing very few men. Contrast this to the Russians. 50,000 people may have died in the Chechen Republic including 5,000 Russian soldiers in similar urban combat. The British and Americans showed that one could fight in an urban environment without destroying everything and still secure the major centers. As George Patton is supposedly quoted, "You don't win wars by dying for your country, you win wars by allowing the other poor bastard to die for his country." Americans and the British can fight in the urban center, in open ground, and on the sea as well as the air.

Vladimir Dvorkin, the head of the Russian Defense Ministry's think tank reflected the thinking of many in the Russian military when he said, "The gap between our capabilities and those of the Americans has been revealed, and it is vast. We are very lucky that Russia has no major enemies at the moment, but the future is impossible to predict, and we must be ready." Mr. Dvorkin lamented that the second Gulf War demonstrated the archaic structure of the Russian military force.

Israeli defense officials expressed similar amazement when they witnessed one of the more powerful Arab countries conquered by what amounted to fewer than three American divisions. Major General Dan Harel told a reporter that he was jealous of the American military. He said, "They have advanced in areas that we were leading in only a few years ago. They have the ability to put everything together in command and control. Our navy and air force have systems. But we have to integrate them." Israelis were impressed that the Americans lost slightly over 100 men whereas the Israelis lost six times as many in the Six Days War. Both friend and foe will study this war for its appropriate lessons.

What the Americans do have is ingenuity. Stephen Ambrose in his many books on World War II continuously observed that under the strain of combat, the American soldiers who were raised in freedom, constantly were able to adapt more freely to conditions on the ground than their German counterparts. Technology is not all that wins wars. It also takes the soldier on the ground to make it work. The American soldier is raised in a world of technology, so a strategy based on technology is second nature and this shows in combat as well. The American soldier brings this strength into battle.

Fred Kaplan details that the origin of both Gulf War victories began in the early 80's. With the advent of digital technology, a new war-fighting doctrine was born. With the defeat suffered in Vietnam, a whole generation of officers determined never to repeat Vietnam's mistakes. Among those were Huba Wass de Czege, who wrote a major revision that broke the Army's previous strategy of attrition warfare, setting up static lines against the enemy's assault, and repulsing it with superior firepower. De Czege began a new strategy that emphasizes lightening strikes behind enemy lines and emphasizing speed. Speed Kills. When the first Gulf War began, many of De Czege's students were part of Norman Schwarzkopf's staff and the Gulf War was a combination of superior firepower matched with feints and the classic deep strike behind Saddam's army, still in Kuwait.

With the advent of smart bombs and their increased use in the combat the military could better target its weapons while employing deception. Increased accuracy also meant fewer civilian causalities. Fred Kaplan said of this strategy, "Operation Desert Storm was really two wars—the air war and the ground war—each fought autonomously and in sequence. Gulf War II was an integrated war, waged simultaneously and in synchronicity, on the ground, at sea, and in the air. The vast majority of air strikes, from Air Force bombers and attack planes as well as Navy fighters, were delivered on Iraqi Republican Guards, in order to ease the path of U.S. Army soldiers and Marines thrusting north to Baghdad." As mentioned previously, synergy of all of the services became a reality. In addition Fred Kaplan stated, "Another new thing, which started in Afghanistan and continued in Iraq, was the systematic inclusion of the so-called "shadow soldiers," the special operations forces. The 1986 Goldwater-Nichols Act, which was best-known for giving new authority to the chairman of the Joint Chiefs of Staff, also made special ops a separate command, with its own budget." The warriors of the night became an integral part of American strategy.

Ralph Peters discussed the possible effect when he theorized, "American agents working with Iraqi intermediaries were able to cut deals with some division commanders (as well as making different deals with other Iraqi officers). Their units would not surrender outright—no white flags would go up—thus preserving their pride and maintaining a degree of unit integrity." We may never know exactly how intelligence and special ops affected the war but their role was indeed valuable.

A pundit recently pointed out that an army that combines the use of Dolphins and satellites is a tough army to beat. This is an army that is capable of using what is available to fight. Americans use old-fashioned "Yankee know-how" in war as effectively as they do in business. The entrepreneurial spirit that exists outside the military has now made its way into the military.

The real lesson to be learned is that we have real enemies and real enemies need to be dealt with—including by military means. When Scholar Victor Hanson wrote, "Arab nationalism created Saddam. He neither asked, needed nor got any help from the United States as he rose to power in the Baath party," he was pointing out the obvious—Many of the present problems in the Middle East are the fault of the local governments. Problems we will have to take care of.

Sanctions were not responsible for the impoverishment of the Iraqi people, Saddam Hussein was. The Kurds, receiving the same per capita share of oil as the rest of Iraq, prospered more than the rest of Iraq. But as Victor Hanson observed, "That may be because the Kurds are not building palaces, new missiles, bunkers and military bases. Nor did the Kurds have a large army, or a secret police organization." Poverty exists in the Middle East as well as the rest of the world simply because corrupt governments robbed their people, but it does not stop many in these countries and some of the Western intelligentsia blaming the West for it. What these countries spend money on is military hardware.

Nor does the fact that the world opposed the United States invasion of Iraq prove the world correct. Victor Hanson concluded, "One difference is that the rest of the world is more risk averse. They would rather tolerate Saddam and the threat he represents than take risks to eliminate his murderous tyranny. Moreover, many people in the rest of the world consider it more important (and a lot safer) to feel right than to do right." Certainly it was in the economic interest of France and Russia to keep Saddam in power as opposed to removing him. What George Bush did was to draw a line in the sand and ask the world to join him.

The war on terror will not be ended by practicing patience but by being bold. Terrorist organizations need state sponsors such as Iraq or Iran to survive. Remove or declaw the sponsor states and you will reduce the terrorist organizations ability to promote terror. Sponsor states are the oxygen that terrorists need. With no home base, there is no ability to strike and what you have is a terrorist network on the run for its very existence.

What Gulf War II showed is that the future war on terrorism will be fought with actual combat, imaginative diplomacy, and through actual subversion of terrorist sponsor states. The combat tactics of Gulf War II demonstrated that the United

States has the capability to either strike with the thunder of armed columns or the lightning speed of special ops operating in the shadows. One can argue whether we needed more troops to pursue our goals or not. I am not a military expert to determine the exact need of an army to win a war but it is obvious that the present campaign was a success. It does not mean that we can't learn from any mistakes made. What is not debatable is that to win the war on terror in the 21st century we will need armed forces that can essentially fight under any and all conditions. Nothing replaces a well-trained soldier carrying out the policies of diplomats; but without the soldier, diplomacy is nothing more than an empty bluff.

13

Reagan's Victory and It's Lesson For Us Today

In the decade when Soviet Communism entered its death throe, the luminaries of the American Left continued to sing its praises. "The Russian system succeeds," opined John Kenneth Galbraith, "because in contrast to Western Industrial economics, it makes full use of its manpower."

"Those in the U.S. who think the Soviet Union is on the verge of economic and social collapse, ready with one small push to go over the brink are…only kidding themselves," said Arthur Schlesinger.

"Can economic command significantly compress and accelerate the growth process?" Lester Thurow inquired rhetorically, in his student textbook, "The remarkable performance of the Soviet Union suggests that it can. In 1920, Russia was but a minor figure in the economic councils of the world. Today it is a country whose economic achievements bear comparison with those of the United States."

While American academicians and literati gushed their praises, a graduate of Eureka State College assessed the situation more accurately. "In an ironic sense, Karl Marx was right," he said, "We are witnessing today a great collapse in the free non-Marxist West, but the home of Marxism-Leninism, the structure that no longer corresponds to its economic base, a society where productive forces are hampered by political ones." "In fact," said President Ronald Reagan, "communism, the 'evil empire was a sad bizarre chapter in human history whose last pages even now are being written."

Peter Schewizer in two books on Reagan's policy on the Soviet Union, wrote, "In early 1982 the President and a few key advisers began mapping out a strategy to attack the fundamental economic and political weakness of the Soviet system.

"We adopted a comprehensive strategy that included economic warfare, to attack Soviet weakness," Casper Weinberger said, "It was a silent campaign working through allies and using other measures." This was a strategy designed to shift the focus of the superpower struggle to the Soviet bloc and to Russia itself.

The directives that defined the policy included:

- NSDD-32, which called for an expanded program of covert support for underground movements resisting Communist rule in Eastern Europe:
- NSDD-56 outlining a strategy of increased economic warfare on the Soviet Empire including restrictions on the availability of critical technologies;
- NSDD-75, which articulated our shift from a posture of co-existence to a policy aimed at radical change within the Soviet Union; and
- NSDD-166, sharply escalating the Afghan war, with the goal of Soviet defeat.

Reversing three decades of containment, the Reaganites fully intended to roll back Soviet gains of the Brezhnev era. During the mid-70's, communism had established African beachheads in Angola and Ethiopia. Nicaragua under the Ortegas gave the Soviets a forward base for the training and supply of anti-American forces throughout the western hemisphere.

The radical Islamic state, which replaced the Pahlavi dynasty in Iran, undercut U.S. influence in the Middle East both economically and politically; and the Soviet invasion of Afghanistan threatened to tilt the balance of power toward Moscow.

High per barrel OPEC prices benefited the radical Arab states and the Soviet Union, whose greatest source of foreign exchange was oil. The Soviets intended to construct a great Siberian pipeline to link Western Europe to their empire in a relationship of dependence. Their goal was the destruction of NATO. The trick was to get Western Europe to finance it.

Meanwhile the Soviet Union continued its aggressive arms buildup. During the Carter presidency, Soviet planners had every reason to believe the correlation of forces was tilting in their direction.

The Reagan counter-offensive concentrated on three crucial fronts:

- The administration's arms build-up used the superiority of American technology to pressure Soviet industry in areas where it could not readily follow The Strategic Defense Initiative was a conspicuous example.

- The Reaganites carried the Cold War to the Soviet Empire, both on its periphery and at its core. Support for the Polish Solidarity movement was important because of the shock waves that it sent through Eastern Europe.

- The United States waged economic war on the Soviets, denying them crucial technology and thwarting the construction of the Siberian pipeline. But the American courtship of Saudi Arabia was the subtlest and least reported form of economic warfare. By assuming defense responsibilities in Saudi Arabia, including the provision of advanced weapons systems, the U.S. broke the OPEC cartel. The Saudis flooded international markets with cheap oil. Declining energy prices not only stimulated the economies of the capitalist West, but also violently undercut the chief source of hard currency for the Soviet Union.

Seen in this light, the Gulf War and present crisis was a logical continuation of Reaganite policies. From the beginning of Ronald Reagan's administration, Soviet leaders understood their opponent better than most of his fellow Americans. U.S. military exercises increased around the European and Asian peripheries of the USSR. The psychological message was clear: appeasement was no longer U.S. policy.

The Reagan administration undertook in cooperation with the Vatican, Sweden and others policies to keep the Polish Solidarity movement afloat. At the same time, CIA Director Bill Casey succeeded in arming the Afghans with the Stinger, an advanced mobile anti-aircraft system, initiating the pattern of attrition, which ultimately forced Soviet withdrawal from Afghanistan.

The Reagan team headed by Bill Casey, Casper Weinberger and Bill Clark initiated one of the most successful foreign policies of the 20th century. The first lesson for American policy we learn from the Reaganite team is that a free society must use national defense and free trade synergistically. Only a powerful America could have persuaded the Saudis to break with the OPEC cartel. Market based energy prices formed the international backdrop of both the Reagan economic recovery and the Soviet economic demise. Force has its own "clearing price." When the free world downgrades its military, the marginal value of force increases in tyrannies throughout the world. In viewing the present crisis, only American strength can change the equation of the Middle East for the good. Bush's economic policies are similar to Reagan's and this will only strengthen the American economy.

Second, a great power acts in its own interest, pushing its allies to act in concert. Multilateral defense schemes recapitulate the disastrous practices of Great Britain and France following World War I. Reagan asserted United States leadership, pushing NATO into accepting the Pershing missiles as a counter to the rapid growth of the Soviets SS-20. As a result, even "neutral" countries like Sweden participated in covert actions, which advanced global victory. The recent actions of the UN demonstrate that multilateral defense will not work unless the United States takes the lead.

Third, the ethical posture of Free World statesmen must be painted on a broad canvass. The Cold War ended without a major war in Europe, and Central Europe was liberated from Soviet domination. But getting there, we allied ourselves with "enemies of our enemies" who were and are not necessarily our friends. This will be no different in the upcoming war on terror.

Finally, technological advance, a specialty of free enterprise systems has become decisive politically. Strategic Defense was the cutting edge of external superiority in weaponry whereas computers, copiers and fax machines were the weapons-of-choice of the block dissidents. The use of the computer and direct satellite can work to undermine countries such as Iran, where the opposition forces are building against the Islamic fundamentalist regime. Strategic Defense strengthens America's ability to protect its interests and allies against rogue states such as North Korea.

The United States can't withdraw its security umbrella and expect the economic arrangements, which prevail there to remain unaffected. A hollow military will increase the marginal value of force among our enemies. It behooves the U.S. to lead, rather than subject its military forces to United Nations multilateralism. Might and right are likelier to converge in the interests of the world's largest free market economy than in an improbable consensus of "United Nations." Reagan's lessons are ours. The Bush team appears to be learning the right lessons from the Reagan era.

BOOK II

Men For Our Century

Editor's note: Very few people know Whitaker Chambers, Friedrich A. Hayek, Herman Kahn or Leslie Groves but these men influenced the 20th century. Chambers was the most prominent witness to the communist infiltration post World War II. When Chambers came forth with his story, Americans were not aware of the nature of the ideology they were fighting. After congressional hearings in which he fingered Alger Hiss as a communist spy, Chambers would write Witness, which described the case. Witness is more than a spy story, in some ways it is an expose of the nature of communism by a brave witness.

Hayek was the leading defender of free market economics in the 20th century. Hayek found himself a lonely voice during the 1930's as Capitalism was supposedly discredited due to the Great Depression. Hayek's influence grew as it became obvious that socialism as an economic theory severely restricted economic freedom while destroying economic growth. Both Ronald Reagan and Margaret Thatcher read Hayek, and their policies were in no small part due to his influence.

Herman Kahn was the real Dr. Strangelove. He would write about nuclear war as if it was just another form of warfare, and concluded that survival was possible. When he was not thinking about the unthinkable, he was predicting a bright future for Americans. How could a man think about the possible end of the world, and at the same time, forecast an American century going into the 21st century? While Kahn wrote about the unthinkable, Leslie Groves assured its arrival. Groves pushed and cajoled a group of American scientists to develop the atomic bomb. Most Americans do not know General Groves but without Groves, the atomic age would not have been created. History will judge whether Groves provided the basis for general peace and stability during the cold war, or was the evil mad general who brought us to the brink of destruction.

1

Whitaker Chambers—A Prophet for Our Times

Whitaker Chambers was a prophet for our times, a prophet never fully understood by either the left or the right. Chambers began his adulthood as a writer for communist controlled journals and then he went underground as a communist spy, a portion of his life that will make his fame and place in history. For most of the 20's and 30's, he, like many intellectuals and writers, believed communism would create a better world. Chambers own change of heart occurred when he realized that the dictatorship of the proletariat was in fact the tyranny of one man, Stalin.

In the 1930's, there was very little counterintelligence so being a Soviet spy was hardly challenging. As one Soviet spy quipped, "If you wore a sign saying "I am a spy, you might still not get arrested." During the Depression, Communism had its own appeal in a country struggling with high unemployment and the apparent collapse of the capitalist state. Chambers was the courier between his Soviet handler and various members of the government, including Alger Hiss. Later as we shall see, Whitaker Chambers and Alger Hiss would be involved in the most publicized and politicized battle of the late 40's.

In 1939, Chambers made his break from the communist party and joined the staff of Henry Luce's Time Empire, which included Life and Fortune. If anything, Chambers was a brilliant writer and his presence on the staff proved controversial, as he would on many occasion overturn and rewrite many of his field reporters' materials-especially, if it dealt with the Soviet Union or communism.

Henry Luce, when he hired Chambers found a kindred spirit. Luce believed in Christianity, big business and the Republican Party. Many of Luce's staff did not share his belief and as Luce wisecracked, "Goddam Republicans can't write."

Chambers and Luce believed in many of the same things, except Chambers never forsake his bohemian—Bolshevik contempt for businessmen. As Chambers moved right, he shared Luce's dislike of the New Deal; and Luce found Chambers to be one of his best writers. Chambers' style included blending a narrative style and argumentative line of reasoning enlivened with catch phrases and quotes from the classics. Chambers was not universally liked in the newsroom as he would produce pieces that showed disdain for communist policies while others in the newsroom preferred "a middle ground" between capitalism and communism. Whether it was the foreign desk or the book or cinema reviews, he threw salvos at the left. Chambers assailed various leftist writers such as Lillian Hellman, Dorothy Parker and John Steinbeck by calling them fellow travelers who wanted "to fight fascism. How should they know that Lenin was the first fascist and that they were cooperating with the party from which the Nazis had borrowed all their important methods and ideas?"

At the end of World War II, he would have conflicts with Teddy White and John Hersey about their stories dealing with Europe and China. When Teddy White wrote a sympathetic piece on Mao, Chambers would change the story. Chambers did not view Mao as some agricultural reformer but a totalitarian thug and predicted that Soviet troops would take over Eastern Europe and establish an Empire that would prove more durable than the defeated Nazis. On both counts, he proved more correct than many of field reporters writing for Time.

After the War, the House of Un American Activities (HUAC) investigated communist spy rings and as evidence mounted that a Soviet spy ring existed within the government—Whitaker Chambers became a reluctant witness. As a Time editor, he knew that communists existed in government because he was a spy. The rub is that if he publicly admitted his communist past in any hearings, his past history of espionage would be public record and put him at risk of being tried for treason. As the hearings progressed, Chambers was dragged in and testified that Alger Hiss was indeed a communist spy along with himself.

Hiss was Ivy League educated and a highly regarded member of the government. A long time bureaucrat, no one truly believed that Hiss was a spy. Sharply dressed and well groomed, Hiss looked the part of a leader and his number one accuser, Whitaker Chambers with bad teeth, overweight and sloppily dressed, proved a contrast in style. The initial impression was that Chambers was the liar and Hiss was the victim of a smear.

Only, Chambers was the one telling the truth and it was Hiss that proved to be the liar. After two trials and months of congressional hearings, Chambers would be vindicated and Hiss would go to jail for perjury. The result was one of the great books of the 20th century, "Witness", in which Chambers detailed this case.

This case launched Richard Nixon's career as he defended Chambers and made him a hero among the conservative wing of the GOP. While Henry Luce knew of Chambers past Communist connections when he hired him for Time, he never knew that Chambers was actually a spy. There were two secrets that Chambers wanted to keep secret. The first was his actual espionage history and the second was his homosexual past. Chambers, like his father, was bisexual and had several same sex relations along with sexual relations with women. It was not uncommon for the party to "arrange party marriages" and Chambers, like other communists, were set up in extra marital arrangements since it represented a rebellion against bourgeois moral values. When Chambers came from the underground, he became a Christian and declared himself "broken of homosexual tendencies." After he married his present wife, Esther, he once said, "that I have lived a blameless and devoted life as husband and father." Chambers insisted that he had mastered his desire when he found God.

When facing off against Hiss in the public hearings and later through court trials, he was afraid that his sexual past would become public—a fate he prepared himself for. As he told his wife, "I tell it now only because, in this case, I stand for truth. Having testified mercilessly against others, it has become my function to testify mercilessly against myself." In the end, Hiss's team did not use this information, only because Hiss was the victim of rumors dealing with his own sexual past. (In the late 40's, homosexuality was a taboo subject for public officials and certainly, this could have swung the case against Chambers and destroyed him as a witness.) What swung the case against Hiss was that Chambers hid various documents that proved that both men were indeed communist spies. Throughout the case, Chambers kept this fact hidden and it was only near the end of the hearings that Chambers released the documents. This evidence convicted Hiss but it also ended Chambers career with Time, which was in its ascendancy. Before the case, Chambers was poised to be one of America's most influential correspondents and editors as part of Luce's Time Empire.

When the case ended, Time did not rehire Chambers and he was set adrift. The case also took a toll on Chambers health as his heart weakened and eventually failed him in 1961. As the 50's progressed, he would still contribute to the conservative movement. In the early 50's Joseph McCarthy was a political force using his anti-communist credentials to push his political career but his reckless attacks undermined his own case. In spite of this, many conservatives defended him. Bill Buckley along with Brent Bozell wrote a book, "McCarthy and his Critics" in which they not only attack his critics but also defended his tactics. Chambers felt otherwise. In Chambers eye, McCarthy's tactics would, in the end, fail and merely discredit the anti-communist movement. He felt that the conservative movement should disown McCarthy but kept much of his criticism to himself.

Chambers and the younger Bill Buckley became good friends but they disagreed on tactics. Chambers felt that new tactics against communism were needed as Stalin passed from the scene. In Chambers eyes, the death of Stalin would change the nature of the cold war and communism. Buckley felt that a frontal attack was needed on the New Deal at home and Communism abroad. Buckley differed from Chambers in both age and experience. Buckley's conservatism was a family heritage whereas Chambers, like many leading conservative intellectuals of the time, came to the right because of his experience with the left.

Buckley obtained notoriety when he published "God and Man at Yale" which became an influential conservative tome. Buckley's theory was that Yale derived its support and heritage from "Christian individualists" and this heritage was being undermined. He would write of his alma mater that Yale was "itself to the task of persuading the sons of these supporters to be atheistic socialists." Buckley's major goal was to establish a conservative magazine to challenge the liberal hegemony of both the media and intellectual movement. In the 1950's, liberalism was the dominant thought and much of the conservative movement was shunted to the sideline. Buckley wanted to change that and wanted Chambers involved in the project.

At this moment as Sam Tanenhaus, Chambers biographer, wrote, "Chambers, on the other hand, was moving further away from the radical right and toward the center." While Buckley and his friends view Eisenhower as nothing more than a moderate Republican who'll keep the New Deal in place, Chambers viewed Eisenhower as the most plausible Republican leader—and there was no other electable candidate. Chambers was also loyal to Richard Nixon, who defended him in his darkest hour whereas other members of the conservative movement distrusted Nixon. Chambers made his peace with the New Deal, which he used to equate with revolution just a decade before. Chambers viewed the Rooseveltian vision as permanent and that conservatives were missing the drift of history.

Chambers wrote, "A conservatism blind to political realities is not a political force or even a twitch, it has become a literary whimsy."

Many of NR's original staff was horrified at this change of heart but Buckley did not want to antagonize Chambers, so he did not press this debate. When National Review debuted, Chambers did not join. Within two years, Chambers would join National Review and he would add his own ideas and influence to the conservative movement. Chambers brought a more ideological social conservative ideal to the movement for he never fully trusted or loved the more libertarian movement side of the conservative movement. While others on the NR staff worshipped Ludwig von Mises, a leading free market libertarian thinker—Chambers neither envied capitalism or found Von Mises appealing. His review of Ayn Rand's book, "Atlas Shrugged" showed his own ambivalent attitude on capitalism. Chambers feared that Rand's vision of a "technological elite" smacked of a totalitarian future that he just escaped from. As he wrote on Rand's atheisms, ""Randian Man, like the Marxian Man, is made the center of a godless world…His tragic fate becomes, without God, more tragic and much lonelier….From almost any page of Atlas Shrugged, a voice can be heard, from painful necessity, commanding: "To a gas chamber—go." For many conservatives, Ayn Rand was a libertarian defender of freedom but Chambers felt Rand's atheistic view undermined her vision of liberty, for without a belief in God, man will find new gods—like Marxism.

Chambers death left a void in the conservative movement. This dour looking man began his life looking for stability and God but found Marx. During his years in the underground, he developed a dislike for secular gods and in religion he found a loving and forgiving God that transcended man's own false gods. Chambers was pessimistic at heart and when he left the communist party, he felt that he had joined the losing side nor did he find much hope for the conservative movement in the long run. His pessimisms proved wrong as Communism joined Nazism in the ash heap of history. He could not have foreseen that Buckley would eventually lay the seed for a conservative renewal, or an optimistic politician named Ronald Reagan would not only prove electable but change America's political direction. He was a firsthand witness to Communism, and exposed those who not only were infected with this virus, but who were also prepared to betray their country for false ideals. He would never live to see the final victory-one that he believed would never come.

2

Herman Kahn—Thinking the Unthinkable

Ronald Reagan wrote of Herman Kahn upon Kahn's death, "Herman Kahn was a futurist who welcomed the future. He brought the lessons of science, history, and humanity to the study of the future and remained confident of mankind's potential for good. All who value independent thinking will mourn the loss of a man whose intellect and enthusiasm embraced so much."

Herman Kahn was the original Dr. Strangelove, a man who spent his time thinking about the unthinkable-nuclear war. During the Cold War, he studied and wrote about nuclear war and its impact as well as the possibility that such a war could be won. For Kahn, it would be as immoral not to think about these possibilities as to be an ostrich with it's head in the sand. Kahn, in his last book, wrote, "soldiers are sometimes more profound about war than philosophers; generals can sometimes articulate national purposes better than statesmen. Similarly, military planners and nuclear strategists ought not to be discredited out of hand. *Many of them understand better than most the 'immorality' of nuclear war—including not preparing for it."*

Kahn was also a futurist, a man who looked into the future. And for a man who spent his life thinking about the possible end of civilization was an optimistic man about our future. His 1982 book, "The Coming Boom" detailed his predictions for the next two decades, which brings us to now. What is amazing is that for the most part, he was correct. Writing in the midst of a serious recession, Kahn correctly predicted the boom that we are still in the midst of. For Kahn, this was a risky proposition since he was writing at a time in which one out of every ten Americans was unemployed, and pundits were blistering Reaganomics. There was no way that Kahn could predict that Reagan's policy would be followed.

Kahn understood the value of the new technology and wrote, "One of the reasons we expect relatively high and sustained growth through the 1980's and 1990's is that a whole host of new technological improvements are now...ripe for large—scale exploitation." Kahn observed that there is normally a lag between the time the new technology is marketed and the point it has a significant impact. Computer technology shortened this period and in the early 80's, individual PCs and Apples were becoming available to the general public. This revolution had the effect of allowing work to essentially be done anywhere. At a time when other developmental models were being promoted, Kahn correctly predicted that the new technology would allow the United States to become the leading source of technological innovation. When many critics were looking to Germany and Japan as their model, Kahn sensed that the next two decades would be ours to control. Ronald Reagan was elected as a result of his optimistic view of America, but in the midst of a recession, Reagan's vision looked antiquated and gloom hung over America. Kahn understood that the new computer technology would change the way we do business and interact with each other. It represented a typical American view that change is good. He foresaw the new biotechnology revolution that would change agriculture, increase yield and have an impact in the development of new pharmaceuticals.

As we left the 70's, America was beset by double-digit inflation and Kahn predicted, "Inflation is more likely than any other single problem to prevent or diminish the impact of the coming boom." Inflation was undermining the average American's earnings and destroying his savings. The Reagan assault on inflation underpinned the coming boom, and his tax cut plans unleashed entrepreneurial activity throughout the economy. Kahn was an early advocate of a simplified tax code with a top rate at 12 percent (which is similar to the present Russian tax codes that is helping to revitalize the present Russian economy.) Kahn understood that the Reagan plan to reduce regulation, tax reduction and anti-inflation emphasis would prove to be basis of upcoming boom.

On foreign affairs, Kahn predicted a movement from a bi-polar to a multi-polar world. While the United States is the lone superpower at the moment, we are seeing a multi power world rising. In Southern Asia, India is starting to stretch its horizons and China is slowly becoming a rival to American interests in Southeast Asia. Both countries have experienced remarkable economic growth over the past decade as both countries opened up their economy. Kahn viewed an alliance between France and Germany as a possible seed for a European super rival and today, there are many in the European Union who seeks rivalry with the United

States. Russia's economic weakness masks a potential superpower reborn. Russia still has nuclear weapons, plenty of material resources including oil and natural gas and finally is gradually moving into a market economy. This could lead to a Russian economic revival and allow Russia to return to World Superpower status.

Kahn viewed such a development as adding stability to the world but warned, "It might contribute to regional instability as various regional adjustments are made to the new constellation of forces." The Middle East is a prime example of this as various Regional powers vie for control of the area and simultaneously work to remove Western influence from the area as Iran is striving to become a nuclear power in its own right. This is adding to instability in the Region, with Iran and Syria now providing aid to various terrorist organizations.

Kahn anticipated this in his last book, "*Thinking about the Unthinkable,*" when he wrote, "If the Great Powers failed to develop active and passive defenses to complement their offensive forces, other countries could buy relatively simple nuclear-weapon systems, and using relatively simple (though perhaps more dangerous) techniques for making these systems invulnerable, could then also claim to be Great Powers. Nuclear threats and nuclear deterrence between a great and a lesser nuclear power would then become two-way streets." Kahn's solution to this dilemma, "would increase the need for strategic defenses...if the Great Powers did possess elaborate strategic defenses capable of protecting them against limited attacks, the smaller powers could not really challenge them"

Strategic defenses are the West's trump card against the various terrorist states that possess nuclear weapons. A workable strategic defense would diminish the incentive for smaller powers to proceeds with nuclear technology or reduce the power of regional terrorists to blackmail their neighbors. Kahn's view is that a multi polar world could be stable but only in the context of a concert of great powers very similar to the famous Concert of Europe in the 19th century engineered by Austrian diplomat Klemons von Metternich. Kahn wrote, "A future multi-polar world would be similar to the balance-of-power system which existed in Europe from 1815 to 1914. It is fair to say that from 1871 until its failure in 1914 through a series of coincidences, deterrence via balance of power kept the peace....A nuclear armed multi-polar world would partake of the aspects of the balance-of-power system that are conductive to international equilibrium while avoiding some of the fatal instabilities." For Kahn, a multi-polar nuclear world dominated by major countries was not to be feared but in the long run is more stable.

Today's war against terror will be the test and possible transition to that multi-power world. With the rise of India and China, the rebuilding of Russia and the establishment of a new Europe, we are seeing the beginning of that world. Whether Kahn's prediction of stability comes true will depend upon the results of the present war against terrorism. Kahn's economic thesis proved correct as the Coming Boom is still with us. His optimistic view of the future was based on the renewal of the American entrepreneurial spirit ignited by the Reagan Administration. Kahn never lived to see his vision come true, but his legacy for America was a realistic view of the world during the nuclear age. His prediction was not a Pollyanna vision, but a practical understanding of America's strength and weakness. The good news was that America's strength was greater than America's weakness. For a man who was considered America's Dr. Strangelove, Kahn proved to be a most optimistic man on our future.

3

F.A. Hayek—An Economist for Freedom

As a disciple of Ludwig Von Mises Austrian School of Economics, Friedrich A. Hayek was an ardent defender of free markets. Throughout his entire life, he debated and fought the socialist thoughts of his era. In the beginning of this century, Socialism was a theory not yet tested. It was not until the Great Depression and the Russian Revolution that Socialism became an attractive economic theory. For many, the Russian Revolution was the spark that would lay waste to Capitalism, and the Great Depression buried the free market as a practical idea whose time as passed. Socialism represented the wave of the future.

F. A. Hayek, like many classical economists, became embattled in the academic world as he was one of the last on the rampart defending free markets. In the depth of the Depression, John Maynard Keynes proposed active government intervention in the economy as a mean to *save Capitalism!* Keynes did not desert the markets, but felt that through government fine-tuning, prosperity could be restored. The "invisible hand" of capitalism had failed and it needed government help to succeed. Others simply lost faith in Capitalism and Keynesian theories offered a safe political avenue to advance socialism. Even in 1930's America, socialism still did not have enough appeal to advance at the ballot box.

This was the world that Hayek inhabited and in 1944, he would write his first tome—"The Road to Serfdom." Hayek's thesis is that socialism will not come all at once in the West but slowly over time. In the beginning of the book, Hayek quoted David Hume, "It is seldom that liberty of any kind is lost all at once." The first thing that changes is psychological. Hayek writes, "The most important change which extensive government control produces is a psychological change, an alteration in the character of the people." This process is a slow process that can alter a people's character over a generation or two. Hayek feared that even in a land in which there is strong tradition of liberty, this spirit could be undermined. When people enjoy the benefits of a paternalistic welfare state, the spirit of liberty is damaged and weakened.

The road to serfdom begins with a desire to find Utopia on earth. "The Road to Serfdom" was written during World War II at a time that we were allied with the Soviet Union to defeat Hitler's Nazi Germany, and many did not see the similarity between Nazism and Communism. Hayek did. He observed that "While progressives in England and elsewhere were still deluding themselves that communism and fascism represented opposite poles, more and more people began to ask themselves whether these new tyrannies were not the outcome of the same tendencies." Many fascists began their political life as socialists such as Benito Mussolini. While historically in the 1920's and early 30's, communists clashed with the Nazi and fascist forces in the street, Hayek remarks, "They competed for the support of the same type of mind and reserved for each other the hatred of the heretic." Hayek's own conclusion was that "democratic socialism, the great utopia of the last few generations, is not unachievable, but that to strive for it produces something so utterly different that few of those now wish it would be prepared to accept the consequences."

Hayek agreed with Lord Acton's philosophy, "Power tends to corrupt and absolute power corrupts absolutely." In a socialist society, Hayek's principle was that "worst get on top." Hayek philosophized, "just as the democratic statesman who sets out to plan economic life will soon be confronted with the alternative of either assuming dictatorial powers or abandoning his plan, so the totalitarian dictator would soon have to choose between disregard of ordinary morals and failure. It is for this reason that the unscrupulous and uninhibited are likely to be more successful in a society tending toward totalitarianism." Brutality pays in a dictatorship. Hitler and Stalin succeeded when others fail because they had no morals and no worries about killing millions to obtain their goals.

Hayek noted that historically in Italy and Germany, socialists were reluctant to run governments, leaving a vacuum on the left for the fascists and Nazis. Even some early English Fabians supported empire, and as George Bernard Shaw quipped, "the world is to the big and powerful states by necessity; and the little ones must come within their borders or be crushed out of existence." Brutality could be seen even within the ranks of some "democratic socialists." Gurcharan Das, an Indian writer, observed that democracy should be in the hand of modest men and women. To exercise power, brutality is required and morality shunted aside.

For Hayek, bigger was not better and he surmised, "We shall not rebuild civilization on a large scale. It is no accident that on the whole there was more beauty and decency to be found in the life of small peoples, and that among the large ones there was more happiness and content in proportion as they had avoided the deadly blight of centralization." Hayek found that democracy could not succeed without a great measure of local self-government, and that it was on the local level that people learned to govern. Hayek feared that "Where the scope of political measures becomes so large that the necessary knowledge is almost exclusively possessed by the bureaucracy, the creative impulses of the private person must flag." In a society that looked for large centralized government, they could lose the services of individual entrepreneurs for one competes with the other.

While the Road to Serfdom represented an early Hayek, the older Hayek in his last book considered Socialism, "the fatal conceit." Hayek perceived that free markets evolved as human activities exceeded the limits of human knowledge and perception. Adam Smith's "invisible hand" detailed how humans serve one another from long distance. Hayek observed about Smith's "invisible hand", "We are led—for example by the pricing system in market exchange—to do things by circumstances of which are largely unanswered and which produce results that we do not intend." Hayek considered free markets a process of evolution that depends upon competition; and it is through continuing competition that more achievements are produced.

Hayek warned against the politics of alienation and stated that a society that attempts to liberate its citizens from the burden of civilization such as hard work, responsibility, risk-taking, saving and honesty as well as honoring promises will lose their political liberty and with it, their economic freedom. Hayek believed in a society governed by the rule of law that protected people's rights, but he was not anarchist.

Hayek's rule considering population is simple. Only a free market society can sustain our present population, and socialism is a threat to the future welfare of society because socialism will not produce the needed growth to sustain population. It was Capitalism that created employment and created the conditions in which people without land could provide for their family. As Hayek concludes, "For the process enabled people to live poorly, and to have children, who otherwise without the opportunity for productive work, could hardly even have grown to maturity and multiplied." Common sense, yes but not universally accepted. Even today, there are people who prefer to restrict population growth as opposed to freeing people's economic freedom. Hayek viewed people as an asset and not a liability.

As for religion, Hayek declares, "But only those religions that have survived are those which support property and the family." In Hayek's view, communism and socialism are a religion and he predicted the demise of both since they were anti-property, anti-family and of course anti-religion. A year after this book was written, the Berlin Wall came crashing down.

Hayek speaks of the irony that many who oppose capitalism only exist because of free markets. For Hayek, these individuals are the great threat to civilization since, while they profess to love liberty, they oppose property rights, contracts, competition, advertising, profit and money itself. They oppose economic rights. Political freedom exists hand in hand with economic freedom, for if all we have is the right to vote with no corresponding economic freedom, then all we will be doing is voting for one set of thieves over another—to see who can steal the most from the federal treasury. Hayek understood the connection.

"The Fatal Conceit" was Hayek's last book, written as he entered his ninth decade. Hayek's influence extended to many in the conservative and libertarian movement. Ronald Reagan and Margaret Thatcher read him and his thinking influenced a whole generation of thinkers. When he wrote the "Road to Serfdom" he stood alone as a defender of free markets in an era when Capitalism was considered passé. Along the way, he won a Nobel Prize and by the time he wrote his last book, his philosophy won out. He was no longer alone.

4

Leslie Groves—Forgotten Man of History

Leslie Groves played the most instrumental role in ending World War II. Put in charge of a top-secret project that would cost two billion dollars, Groves pushed some of America's brilliant minds to develop the ultimate weapon—the Atomic bomb.

Born on a steamy day in August in 1896, Groves entered West Point after one year at the University of Washington and two years at MIT. Upon his graduation from West Point, Groves continued his education in an engineer's school at Camp Humphreys (Fort Belvoir), Virginia between 1918 and 1921, with time out for brief services in France. Over the next decade, he served in San Francisco, Hawaii, Delaware, and Nicaragua. In 1936, he graduated from the Command and General Staff school in Fort Leavenworth, Kansas. And from the Army War College in 1939, he immediately joined the General Staff in Washington, D.C.

Groves engineer's prowess was given an early test as he oversaw the construction of the Pentagon, the world's largest office building. In 1942, Groves was put in charge of the Manhattan Project. One of his first decisions was to appoint J. Robert Oppenheimer to be the director of the Los Alamos National Laboratory. When Groves was appointed to the Manhattan Project, he was dubious of success and tried to get himself removed. Like most military officers, he wanted to be in the thick of battle overseas but like a good solider, he accepted his new duty. Groves decided to overcome his own dubious attitude and make the project work. Promoted to brigadier General, Groves began his work. (The promotion was given to Groves to allow him better to deal with the senior scientists on the project from a position of strength.)

Groves pushed the War Production Board for the highest-priority rating for the project and when the board turned him down at first, he threatened to go over the board's head to the President, directly. The bluff worked. Groves then arranged it so that he would be given a free hand in dealing with the War Department, and his straight shooting and forceful manner was established early. This approach became familiar to the scientific staff and was not always appreciated. He recruited in addition of Oppenheimer, David Bohm, Leo Szilard, Eugene Wigner, Rudolf Peierls, Otto Frisch, Felix Block, Niels Bohr, Enrico Fermi and Edward Teller among others. It would take a strong personality to deal with this all-star talent. Richard Rhodes, author of *The Making of the Atomic Bomb*, wrote, "The brilliant engineer who commanded [the Manhattan Project] has never had his due. Groves finally emerges as the historic, tough, larger-than-life leader who made the atomic bomb happen and gave shape to the atomic age."

Much of his budget came through blind appropriations and he was responsible for a work force that reached 125,000 at its zenith, all this conducted in secrecy. This included a large number of civilian scientists and technicians working on the project. The project proved to be a triumph as the first successful atomic bomb was blasted on July 16, 1945, at Los Alamogordo, New Mexico.

By the time the bomb was ready, Germany had surrendered and only Japan was left to fight. Leo Szilard and James Franck circulated a petition among the staff, opposing the use of the bomb. Groves fought this effort and his advice to Harry S. Truman was to use the bomb. Groves stated of Truman's final decision, "As far as I was concerned, his decision was one of noninterference—basically, a decision not to upset the existing plans." It was as if the bomb was preordained to be used. The opponents feared that such a bomb with its massive destructive power could end civilization and that it would eventually be used on a massive scale. They wanted to short-circuit the nuclear age. With the invasion of Japan being prepared and a million American casualties being predicted, Groves and others looked at the bomb as a means of shortening the war. Stanley Goldberg, a historian, felt that Groves pushed for the bomb to be dropped in small part due to justifying the cost. Goldberg feels that both shortening the war and justifying the cost played equal roles in Groves' own opinion in advising the President to drop the bomb.

There were feelers from some members of the Japanese government beginning in July through the Russians for peace terms while other members of the Japanese government prepared for a final stand on the island that would have included civilians. An invasion of Japan meant a fight to the death. Even as the Emperor announced Japan's surrender to the Japanese over the radio, there was an attempted coup to stop the broadcast. The bomb ended the war and as they say, the rest is history.

Groves continued to serve as the head of the atomic establishment until January, 1947, before moving on to Chief of the Special Weapons Project. He retired in 1948, and worked as the Vice President of Sperry Rand Corporation until 1961. He passed away in 1970 in Washington. Groves was the driving force that ensured that the bomb was created and used. A brusque man, he pushed the cream of the American scientists corps to finish a project that some wanted to end prematurely as the time approached to use the bomb. While Oppenheimer was the scientific mind behind the bomb, Groves was the managerial genius. Groves has been a forgotten man in history, and on his shoulders the atomic age began in earnest.

BOOK III

The New South:
A Reappraisal.

Editor's note: This was originally written after Senator Lott praised Strom Thurmond's segregationist past. It ended Lott's career but as a man who was raised in Virginia, I have a little understanding of the old South and how it has changed. Through the career of two Senators, we can see how the south has grown. Strom Thurmond was an old fashioned segregationist who spent most of his career fighting Civil Rights, but by the time he retired at the age of 100—he surrendered to the inevitable. Phil Gramm was one of the Senate's leading advocates of free markets and what Gramm showed is that one could be a southern conservative without being a southern bigot. A tough defender of free market economics, Gramm began his career as a Jeffersonian Democrat but converted, becoming a Reagan Republican—which was essentially the same thing. Gramm showed the maturity and growth of Southern Thought.

1

The Overture—The New South

I was raised in Northern Virginia, spending my formative years there. It could easily be said that Northern Virginia is not really part of the south but a mere addition of Washington D.C.; but technically speaking, I lived in the South. I went to JEB Stuart High School and it was rumored that under the football stadium existed an old confederate grave. You can't get much more southerner than that. There are two South's. The first South is a romanticized place that never existed but is forever remembered. A society that was class based with the plantation owners at the top followed by the common farmer, who barely scratched out a living and finally, African—American slaves—without whom there were be no Southern economy or southern culture. "Gone With the Wind" was the perfect description of the old South that is forever idealized.

The second South is a more progressive south, which is struggling with its racist past and moving forward to a new future. The new South is a fast growing area in which many now move to and live. My brother, an ophthalmologist in Greenville, South Carolina, told me of a retired patient, originally from Iowa. When my brother asked his patient why he moved to South Carolina, the man responded, "Winters are too cold in Iowa." Weather is the first attraction of the South—mild or no winters, sunshine and plenty of Ocean front property.

My rant on the South was inspired by an interview that I read with Michael Graham. Graham's major point is that we have all become Southerners or "Redneck." Graham has no romantic love for the old South or the Jim Crow era. On the contrary, he fears that many of the racist nonsense that pervaded the old Dixiecrats are now becoming the staple for intellectual elites and many liberals as well.

Michael Graham observed that to an old Southerner, race mattered. Free Speech was something that was okay, as long as you said the right thing. As Graham stated, "free speech was dangerous, spread by "outside agitators" who never learned the southern speech code: if you can't say something nice…drink." Today, it is the political left that cares about race. As Graham observed, "Neighbors that I know live in a modern, liberal America where Ivy League colleges are building segregated housing because, race matters. I actually heard one modern defender of segregated public schools (black-only academies) say 'black people learn differently from white people.' Gee, I haven't heard that since I was 12—from a Klan member!" Graham laments, "On many college campuses, conservative papers are burned on a regularly basis, and evangelical Christians are mocked by liberal elites who wear healing crystals, have conversations with trees and watch John Edwards—TV psychic."

The South is turning Republican, or we should see, the South is becoming a region that is competitive. When I was growing up, to be a southerner was to be a Democrat. Republicans were equated with "Damn Yankees" and the South was essentially a one party state.

Today, as Graham observed, "to be a Republican, you have to believe in something. To be a Democrat you have to be something—a union member, education bureaucrat, part of an ethnic minority, etc." The South is slowly becoming an intellectual oasis in which beliefs mean something. Ideas do matter but in the South, they always did. "State Rights" was not a mere slogan but a means to buttress the old order. Of course, the irony is that many Dixiecrats favored state rights against federal encroachment but they were very much leftist in local politics. To support a segregationist state by law, you had to trample upon peoples rights by government edict.

Old southern politicians use the power of government to interfere with the private right of association. The reality is that Jim Crow laws imposed segregation on private business including hotels, restaurants and even bathrooms by government edict. Interracial marriages were forbidden and Jim Crow laws represented direct governmental interference in a person's private life. The end of the old Segregation South represented the first breath of freedom for many blacks, and even many whites who owned businesses could now sell to whom they wished, not having to forbid African—Americans from patronizing their establishments. Today, the left is now playing the race card. Graham reflected upon a story in the Washington Post when he told National Review Online, "Absolutely! One of my favorite stories is a *Washington Post* article written by Natalie Hopkinson, a black *Post* staffer who was upset that so many white people were moving into her neighborhood. D.C. is "Chocolate City," she insisted, and white people were ruining it by moving in.' From our perspective,' she wrote, "integration is overrated…We not only have to invest in the inner city, but we can't let white people beat us to it.' Her arguments could have come straight from the minutes of a "White Citizens Council" meeting from the 1960s, steeped as it was in racism, segregation, and implied intimidation ("We don't want your kind 'round here"). And the *Post* ran it!"

Today it is the South that is providing the intellectual fire to the conservative revolution. Ronald Reagan owed his victory to the South and it was southern politicians that provided the margin to pass his tax reduction plans. Southern professor Newt Gingrich pushed a freedom-oriented agenda in the 90's that is now the staple of former Texas governor George W. Bush. Dick Armey and Phil Gramm were important defenders of free market policies in Congress and it was Phil Gramm's desertion of his Democratic roots that allowed Reagan his legislative victories. The irony is that it is southern politicians that were providing the basis of more economic freedom, and it is the Democratic left that is the biggest offender in its opposition of more economic freedom.

The Bush brothers are the new southerners. George W. was born in the North but he was raised in Texas and his mannerism is southern. His brother, Jeb Bush, is similar in both mannerism and beliefs. The South is now embracing a new generation of northerners and turning them into southerners. Hell, Nascar is the fastest growing sport in the United States. A sport that was born out of slick drivers avoiding the law while transporting moonshine on back southern roads is now a multi-billion dollar business.

Finally, the South is the most integrated region of the nation. Blacks make up nearly one—third of the population and in Texas and Florida, the Hispanic population is the fastest growing demographic. In my state of Iowa, African—Americans make up less than 3% of the population but in the South, true diversity is everyday reality at the local mall or the grocery stores.

What can we conclude? The South has been undergoing changes that are slowly affecting the rest of the nation. There is a new generation of conservative politician that eschews race and even the old racists or segregationist politicians have long made their own peace with the Civil Rights movement. Lindsey Graham recently replaced Strom Thurmond and this change is symbolic. Old Strom was one of the biggest segregationists in Congress, yet he even bolted the Democratic

Party in 1948 to pursue his own presidential candidacy. Graham is a new conservative where race is not the main vehicle of his candidacy but installation of more free market economy at home and strong defense abroad is. The new South is no longer whistling Dixie.

2

Strom Thurmond

Sue Logue was the only woman in South Carolina ever to be sent to the chair but not before she met a circuit court judge. She sat in the back seat of the Judge's car, awaiting her fate. The judge joined her and the two made love before Logue was sent to the chair. What a lively final meal. And Strom Thurmond demonstrated the one quality that he had throughout his life, his love for the opposite sex. Thurmond has survived a century and was America's most colorful politician—who maintained many amorous adventures, even late in life.

Reporter Mark Steyn tells of his first and only meeting of Thurmond four years ago. During the Clinton impeachment trial, the reporter was thrown between Thurmond and California Senator Barbara Boxer. Thurmond cast his eye upon the petite liberal brunette and her political affiliations did not seem to matter. As Steyn writes, "I was squashed between the two for about five seconds when I became aware that my elbow was being affectionately caressed by Strom. Presumably he'd mistaken my dainty arm for Barbara's, but who knows? But what a great country. In how many other national legislatures can a guy just wander in off the street and find himself in a tri partisan squeeze being petted by a 97-year-old senator?" Steyn observed that when the chief justice declared a 15 minute recess, Thurmond strolled up to the President's two lady lawyers and patted them down, stroked their elbows and kept hold of them until the gavel ended the recess. Cheryl Mills, an African-America, looked confused and probably was unsure how to react. Or maybe she wondered how a former segregationist would find her attractive enough to be hit upon. Call it Thurmond's attempt at real integration. Meanwhile, his 41-year old girlfriend stared at the events unfolding in front of her. Even as he approached the century mark, he was still hitting on women.

In 1923, it was rumored though never confirmed, that ole Strom fathered a child by a black woman. The best that one can say about Thurmond is that his roman-

85

tic adventures outshined his legislative accomplishments. Of course, Thurmond had romantic adventures that would make most politicians envious. As Steyn writes, "Considering that only 100 folks get to be senator out of a talent pool of almost 300 million, there's a lot of mediocrities in there." At the age of 100 and nearly senile, Thurmond still was sharper than many of his colleagues. Steyn observed, "On the basis of the few exchanges I had with him at the trial, Strom seemed one of the sharper guys: Jim Jeffords is a third his age, but try getting a coherent sentence out of Jim when his aides aren't around."

James Strom Thurmond was born on December 5,1902 and was a graduate from Clemson College in 1923. Mr. Thurmond was born before the Wright brothers flew their first plane, born in an era where flying was merely fiction in Jules Verne's book, to retiring when we were reaching the moon, making Verne's fiction a reality.

He was a farmer, teacher and athletic coach until 1929, when he became superintendent of education and finished his law education before joining the board in 1930. In 1933, he was elected to the South Carolina bar, preceding his election to the Eleventh Circuit judgeship. He served in the Army and participated in D-Day, then served in the Pacific when the war ended. He was elected Governor in 1946. While Governor, he left the Democrat party briefly to form the Dixiecrats and run for President. This movement was the result of Truman's support of Civil Rights. Like other southern politicians, he was a segregationist and Truman's support of Civil Rights did not sit well with him. He managed to carry four states but did not deny Truman his election to the Presidency. In 1950, he failed to obtain the Senate seat but in 1954, he won a write in election against Edgar Brown becoming the only candidate to ever win a write in vote for a national office until Linda Smith of Washington State in recent years. Thurmond's Senate career led to service on many important committees but his Senate career was mired in support of the southern way of life. He originated the Southern Manifesto against the 1954 Supreme Court desegregation laws and held the longest filibuster in Senate history when he spoke against the 1957 Civil Rights act. Thurmond joined the Republican Party in 1964 and became a linchpin in Nixon's southern strategy in the 1968 election. He remarried in 1968, Nancy Janice Moore who was 40 years younger than Thurmond, showing the man still had the stuff. (His first wife died of cancer eight years earlier.) She had four children with ole Thurmond before divorcing him in 1991.

Thurmond's major accomplishment was to live to 100 as a United States Senator. It could be said that he accepted the integration that he opposed with passionate zeal. He hired African-American staffers and if nothing else, he gave the signal that the battle was over. Going from a man who left the Democratic Party to protest Truman's Civil Rights cause and leading the fight against integration in the Senate, to a man who made the peace with the movement he opposed—even if he never truly accepted the result. He lived through the Jim Crow era and presided over its death. He surrendered to the inevitable.

3

Phil Gramm—The True Southern Rebel

If Strom Thurmond represented a more racist past in the South, Phil Gramm was part of a new generation of southerners that accepted the gains of the Civil Rights Movement. Gramm, born in Georgia, was the son of a working mom and disabled father who died when he was just a teenager. Gramm's early life did not show the potential of an academic star as he repeated the 3rd and 7th grades. His mother sent him off to a military academy, where he finally found his stride with his schoolwork.

From there he went on to University of Georgia and then completed his Doctrinaire. It was at Texas A & M where Professor Gramm made his mark as a free market advocate. At a time when Keynesian theory reigned supreme at most economic departments, Texas A & M was going in the opposite direction by training advocates of classical free market with Gramm being a part of that team.

Texas A & M was one of the few schools in the late 60's and early 70's that were considered bastions of free market thinking, and while most economists were *learning about the imperfection of the market, students of Gramm and others were learning that maybe government was not always the solution to every problem.* They were the counter revolutionaries of the economic world.

In the 1970's, an economic crisis hit the Western world and the dominant economic class had no answer though Gramm and others did. In 1975, Phil Gramm lectured the Board of Governors of the Saint Louis Federal Reserve Bank about the rampant inflation that existed at the time. "We are today experiencing the most prolonged period of rapid inflation in the history of the United States," he declared. According to Gramm, this inflation spread over a decade was without precedent. Gramm predicted that inflation would get worse and described what would later be called stagflation. No real growth was combined with high inflation, contrary to what Keynesian economists predicted.

Phil Gramm opposed the wage and price controls of Richard Nixon and felt that the Ford Administration was demonizing workers and business instead of looking into the mirror. Gramm noticed that the Federal anti-inflation laws were a fraud and stated that only by slowing the growth of money and government—could inflation be eliminated. It was here that Gramm showed his true nature, Jeffersonian Democrat—a believer of limited government. Such a Democrat has long since been considered extinct. It should be pointed out that to be a Southerner was to be a Democrat but the local Democrats were not true believers of free market, at least on a local level.

To be a supporter of segregation and to preserve the old Jim Crow reign, a politician had to believe in extensive government power to separate races. Translated, a government was duty bound to interfere with free right of association on a local basis and that hardly fit Gramm's own philosophy. When the Ford administration contacted Gramm about working on an energy program, he told the staffer that his solution was simply to forget about spending money on designing a federal energy program and allow the market to work. There was no need for a Government energy program, and Gramm would have to wait until the Reagan administration to finally see his vision acted upon.

Gramm was ahead of his time not only about inflation but taxes as well. When a Kansas City Republican city councilman first head of the term, "Supply side economics" in the early 80's, his first thought flashed back to a speech by Gramm he heard years early. The councilman told Gramm's biographer, Richard Nadler, that Gramm explained the concept to him long before it became a popular idea.

Gramm's first foray into politics was a disaster as Lloyd Bentson swamped him in the Democratic primary in 1976, but he would win a congressional seat two years later. In the House, Gramm quickly showed what kind of Democrat he was. He found himself at odds with his own party, and was part of coalition of conservative Democrats that would help strengthen the Republican hand. But it would be under the Reagan era that he would blossom as a legislator. The professor would soon learn to be a masterful politician. The Democrats ploy in dealing with this rebel was first appeasement as they allowed him on the budget committee. The goal was to keep an eye on Gramm and control his impulses. For many southern Democrats, the ploy usually worked. Give the southerner a key seat and allow him to slip home some bacon to the home folks. Democrats like Sam Nunn or Charles Stenholm would talk about their conservative beliefs at home while basically allowing the Democrat left do what they wanted in Washington.

When Reagan came to town, Gramm met the President whose ideas closely resembled his own positions. Gramm quickly put together a coalition of Boll Weevil Democrats and gave Reagan his first major victories in 1981. He led the charge for budget restraint and played a key role in Reagan tax cuts. Gramm did not compromise his beliefs and eventually was cut from the budget committee. It was here that Gramm changed the political dynamic in another way. Representing a Democratic district, Gramm decided to switch parties. He convinced the Texas governor to allow a special election and Gramm ran as a Republican. He did not just switch but allowed his constituents to decide his fate. He won.

From this point, his influence grew even more. He had voter support for his switch and he now welded new influence, as he became the poster boy for the new Republican Party. By leaving the Democratic Party, he encouraged others to follow and now set his sight on the Senate. In 1984, he proved to be a bulldog in winning his seat. In one of the dirtier campaigns, Gramm gave as good as he got. When his opponent complained about a particular ad, he simply doubled his buy of the ad.

After pushing the Reagan tax cuts, Gramm designed and got passed the Gramm-Rudman-Hollings Act, which provided Congress the mechanism to reduce the budget deficit. Under the Act, the budget deficit dramatically went down in the late 80's. But the Act was undermined by the 1990 recession and George Bush's compromise with Congressional Democrats. The Act was dead and what control that existed, died at the same time.

Gramm would prove once again that he was more than equal to the task when it came to winning political battles. He opposed the Clinton health care plan by opposing its more socialistic approach and proposing a more free market approach such as Medical Savings Accounts. Working tirelessly, Gramm foiled Clinton's attempt to socialize nearly 14% of the economy and turn the American health system into a Canadian version. Clinton's plan died and Gramm once again influenced the debate.

Gramm proved to be one of the most effective legislators over the past two decades when he retired from the Senate and his influence will be missed.

But what made him effective was not just his skills but also his principle. Gramm first began with solid ideas and then found ways to make them work. On taxes, he understood the need to reduce marginal tax rates. When Gramm joined Congress, the top tax rate was 70% and when he left it was 39%. Gramm was a supporter of the flat tax for he felt that it was fairer and more productive for the cost of producing tax shelters is inefficient investment. While he did not ever get a flat tax passed, his version of reduced marginal tax rates is now considered gospel. Even Clinton refused to undo the Reagan revolution. For Gramm, lowering marginal tax rates encouraged people to get out of tax dodges and place their income into more productive investments. Over the past two decades of lowering tax rates, the taxes paid by the wealthy actually increased. The top five percent of taxpayers actually paid 44.1% of all income tax, a 23% increase from the Carter era.

Gramm led the fight to balance the budget and his effort paid off in the late 90's with a surplus even though the recent economic slowdown along with the war on terror has produced new deficits. In the 80's Gramm was a tireless supporter of the Reagan doctrine of supporting freedom fighters whether they lived in Nicaragua or Afghanistan. Again, Gramm's foreign policy was more right than wrong. He was a supporter of those policies that produced the eventual victory in the Cold War.

Gramm was one of the key legislators who helped pass the Reagan tax cuts in the early 80's, and we have witnessed a two-decade plus economic prosperity as a result. Gramm helped move the South from a one party region to a competitive two party system where Republicans compete on an equal basis with Democrats. If nothing else, he proved a Southerner could be a conservative and not be a racist.

Gramm's final legacy is that many of the ideas he taught in the 70's are now considered dominant ideas not just in America but also throughout the world. Free market ideas are now competitive with the liberal Keynesian ideals that swayed over most schools of economics when Gramm taught. Gramm proved to be a statesman, the highest compliment that could be paid to a politician.

BOOK IV

Thoughts on God

Editor's note: During Christmas 2002, thoughts cascaded through my fevered mind. Christmas is the time when we occasionally think about God amid the materialism that exists. Even the materialism itself can be representative of the true spirit of Christmas. Enjoy.

1

Christmas Reminds Us of God

A stone mortuary box bearing the Aramaic inscription, "James, son of Joseph, brother of Jesus" is found and it is said to have contained the bones of James, brother of Jesus of Nazareth. James was an early Christian leader in Jerusalem and was stoned to death as a result. While references to Christ outside the Bible are rare, they do exist along with James. Jewish historian Josephus writes of James as "the brother of Jesus who was called the Christ/Messiah." For the true believer, this discovery does not matter since it is faith that drives a Christian's belief in God. As Jesus tells Thomas the doubter, "blessed are those who believe but not have seen." The apostle Thomas had to physically touch Jesus' scars before he believed. We do not have the ability to physically touch Jesus' scars; all we are left with is faith.

Little miracles like the discovery of the stone mortuary is God's little way of reminding us of His existence to a World that really wants to forget. Even today, Christians are martyred in Nigeria, Sudan, Pakistan and China, and the gory stories of Christians being led to the Lions in ancient Rome still happen. Most everyone agrees that Jesus of Nazareth existed as a historical person and certainly the stone box does not prove that Jesus is the Son of God, only that his brother lived.

The birth of Christ was God's little joke on us. Here was the Messiah, the Son of God, born in a manger, at the peripheral of a great empire. Palestine was hardly considered a plum assignment and I could imagine that Pontius Pilate was hoping to get his tour of duty over with and get back to Rome, where everything was happening. Augustus Caesar was King and God over the Mediterranean and the Roman Empire was close to its apex. Peace reigned over the Empire and Caesar could watch over his domain and see that it was good. The Republic died in the aftermath of a Civil War and now peace and prosperity ruled over all.

Three wise men, maybe Babylonian astrologers, made their way to Jesus. Following a star, they came upon the Christ child and presented their expensive gifts of gold, frankincense and myrrh to this child. How strange it must have seemed to Mary and Joseph to have these men worship their child. It was the rich coming to the lowly and acknowledging their place. The magi prostrated themselves in the presence of greatness.

During the first Christmas of World War I, it would appear that brothers were indeed fighting brothers. Kaiser Wilhelm was related to both the Czar and the King of England and as one German told his British counterpart, "We're Saxons; you're Anglo-Saxons." There was a cultural bond, even religious affinities between the enemies located 70 yards apart. In 1914, a miracle occurred as the voices singing "Stille Nacht, helige Nacht" filled no man's land. German troops, singing Silent Night and lighting their trees, risked death as they appeared from the trenches. British soldiers, curious, crawled out of their trenches to see what was happening. They saw the enemy and made contact. For one brief day, war was no more. For 24 hours, the power of Christ shined through as both sides enjoyed Christmas. Soccer was played and acquaintances made. What began as maybe a break to collect the dead became something more. It appeared across a front that existed for more than 300 miles, a moment of respite from the horror that was World War I. But the miracle ended and man's basic nature returned. The military discipline returned on December 26th and the fighting resumed. There would not be another respite until the armistice was signed, ending the conflict.

The World wars of the 20th century if nothing else, show what happens when men try to replace God. World War II was the war of the Anti Christ. Hitler began his crusade to eliminate the Jews and it was as if, he would wipe out the memory of God's people. It was man's affront to God to attempt the elimination of His chosen people. The Jewish people have been History's wanderers, forever seeking a place to rest and call their own. When they waited in the desert for 40 years after their escape from Egypt, they always had but one thing on their mind—their own homeland. It is the dream of all people to have a place to claim as their own. After the mighty Romans destroyed Jerusalem, the Jewish people were left adrift—becoming the target of the dominant culture they resided in. The German people paid for Hitler's sin but even today, the affront continues. Israel stands one war away from extinction. Even throughout Europe today there is a rise of anti-Semitism with its people hoping to help Israel become extinct.

"When Saul of Tarsus set out on his journey to Damascus, the whole world lay in bondage. There was one state, and it was Rome. There was one master for it all, and he was Tiberius" so began the late Vermont Royster's annual editorials run in the Wall Street Journal on Christmas Eve. Royster explained his editorial was not about theology but politics. In Royster's mind, Caesar and his centurions "were metaphors for modern oppressors, and it was not hard to see that his references were to Stalin, the master of the gulag. Throughout the centuries, freedom has been the one entity continuously deprived. Jesus told us "Render unto Caesar the things which are Caesar's and unto God the things that are God's." Jesus's message was straightforward, there are things that are the purview of God and man cannot interfere or deny. Christianity reminds us that there are matters even more important than ourselves and that even our rulers are under the power of God. Caesar may have his place, but it is to rule not dominate. Caesar can't be God.

It is at Christmas that we need to remind ourselves that a Jewish carpenter was sent to Earth to bring a message of hope and peace. I sit in a Mobile home, leading a Christmas worship services to small group. The piano player's mother just died the night before and somehow, she is both sad and relieved. She is saddened that her mother died but throughout her life, her mother tormented her—a victim of verbal abuse. She seeks her solace in these church services. Her friend suffers from shoulder ailments and another woman is finally back on her feet after a period of unemployment. In this Church, the worshipers are mere reflections of humanity as a whole, broken and seeking the light. For them, this service is that light. It is the end of the year and the light shines into the New Year as we all hope for better days. God's message to us—Love, hope and redemption are all within our grasp. All we have to do is believe.

2

A Christmas Carol

It is said every year; the commercialization of Christmas is terrible. Personally, I do not buy into that philosophy that somehow, giving of gifts is evil and to refrain from Christmas is not much different from how Charles Dickens' Scrooge celebrated Christmas.

For many, Christmas is representative of the greed that consumes modern day America. Somehow to participate in Christmas is to be materialistic, that you miss the real reason for Christmas, the birth of Christ. Christianity is far from hostile towards business and while Jesus does warn against greed, he does not necessarily condemn people with money. Scrooge, himself, is the ultimate symbol of greed but for Scrooge, money was something to be collected and to hoard—not to be spent. Scrooge failed to spend money on himself much less his own business. Scrooge does not spend money on his office, his home or his workers. When Bob Crachett wanted to add an extra coal to keep his office warm, he was turned down.

Charles Dickens writes about Scrooge's home, "It was a very low fire indeed; nothing on such a bitter night. He was obliged to sit close to it, and brood over it, before he could extract the least sensation of warmth from such a handful of fuel. The fireplace was an old one, built by some Dutch merchant long ago, and paved all round with quaint Dutch tiles, designed to illustrate the Scriptures." Scrooge lived in an antiquated home and did not even spend money to keep his own home warm. He denies himself the joy of his own income. Money was merely a scorecard to show his success and Scrooge's selfishness applied even to himself. It is said that charity begins at home and the man who can't share with himself is not very likely to share with others.

Christian thoughts fuel a thriving economy, for business depends upon truth and moral behavior. The recent Wall Street swoon is as much a loss of confidence in the truth of many analysts as anything else. Without trust, market economy can't function. Contrast Scrooge with his nephew Fred, who spends on Christmas and enjoys the gaiety of the holidays. Even the Crachetts celebrate Christmas with their meager savings for money is no object in rejoicing the birth of Christ. For Scrooge, he lived a business life that was more amoral than moral. To him, business was business but as Marley reminds him, "Mankind was our business." A businessman must serve his customer or he will not be successful.

Christmas represents the universal message of peace and forgiveness and you do not need to be a believer in Christianity to buy into these virtues. "A Christmas Carol" is a story of giving and receiving, of redemption and reclamation. The spirits seek to reclaim Scrooge's immortal soul and reform the previously selfish man, whose only thoughts never extended beyond his nose.

It is at Christmas, that we give of ourselves to others. It is the season that we give each other gifts, to show our love for significant others, for our friends and for our spouses and children. Jesus' birth was a gift to mankind, a gift we can never pay back. Three kings arrive from the East with their own gifts of gold, frankincense and myrrh for the new King. Christmas is the symbolic season of unconditional love and giving. A friend of mine once warned me that when lovers or friends begin to keep score, the relationship is soon over. Giving should be unconditional if you love someone, and you should be as appreciative when receiving a gift from others. Giving is a form of showing love and how much you value your relationship with others. Somehow, the world would be poorer and not just materially without Christmas.

As for Scrooge, he was redeemed. He learns his lesson well as Dickens writes, "Scrooge was better than his word. He did it all and infinitely more; and to Tiny Tim who did not die, he was a second father. He became as good a friend, as good a master, and as good a man as the good old city knew…it was always said of him, that he knew how to keep Christmas well, if any man possessed the knowledge."

His change is what Christianity represents. He begins to invest in his business, both in the office by allowing Crachett to use more coal to heat the place and raising Crachett's salary. Christianity is about second chances, third chances, fourth chances and unlimited chances. It is about giving and receiving. Christmas represents those qualities as we seek love and forgiveness from those who are closest to us. It is the spirit of the season that warms us. For a Christian, we can never repay the debt of our Father, who sent his only Son to break the power of sin. So, sometimes we can't repay the debt that others have given to us in the past. What we can do is to share our bounty with others, beginning with those who are the closet. Charity begins at home.

3

Cultural Catholics

The pull of Catholicism appears to be strong even among those of us who have "left her grasp." During a recent discussion with a Methodist Minister, we talked about the phenomenon in which Catholic tradition maintains a strong hold over those who leave the flock and who continue to act the part of being Catholic even though they may quit believing. If a Methodist leaves the church, the Methodist disappears. There is no "cultural Methodist" but there are those who still cling to their Catholicism even after they leave. They are the cultural Catholics.

Writer Michele Catalano wrote, "It's the season of Lent, that time in between Ash Wednesday and Easter when I feel the most guilt about leaving Catholicism. Now, guilt comes with being Catholic. It's instilled in you from an early age, honed and perfected until you become one with it. And someday, should you choose to leave the church, denounce its teaching and have nothing to do with organized religion whatsoever, you will still have the guilt. It's forever."

Michele tells of how she remembers thinking as a young girl, "God will punish you, and God will punish you." Ms. Catalano, an atheist, still raises her children within the Church. She wrote, "I think kids do need some kind of religion. It's comforting for them to have that feeling that someone up there is looking out for them, that there's someone listening to them and trying hard to answer their prayers, that there is a heaven where all their relatives and puppies go when they die and it is a better place than earth." Her quote reminds me of a discussion I had with a friend in the early 80's. The gentleman spend the first 38 years of life without believing in God but when I asked how he raised his own children, he responded, "I allowed my wife, who was very religious, to take the children to Church. I did not want my children to feel my loneliness." It was this emptiness that led him back to God and the church that his wife attended.

Michele Catalano stated that she never got over the guilt and anxiety of the possibility of "wronging the god I didn't believe in." A Jewish friend of mine once told me that only God could come up with the Ten Commandments. The simplicity of the Ten Commandments paints a picture of black and white that we spend a lifetime avoiding. We humans use legalese to defend our actions. Words like "white lies" represent a society that attempts to split the difference but God has always demanded more.

Roman Catholics have their own institution that acts independently of society as a whole and it is this institution that strengthens the average Catholic. Many Catholic boys and girls find themselves being taught in Catholic schools, and Catholic charities already act as an alternative religious welfare state to take care of those who fall through the cracks. These institutions give Catholics an identity that escapes most Protestants.

The Church's 2,000-year tradition provides an anchor that allows the Church to speak with authority on a wide variety of issues and the institution gives Catholics a refuge from the world. The Church simultaneously stands apart from society while involving itself in society. That is why Catholics, even lapsed Catholics, cannot escape its clutches. Those of us who left the Church either for other Churches or religion altogether are still in awe of the Mother Church. Maybe even with all the imperfections and scandals that have rocked and still rock the church, the Church still stands, for it is impervious to the machinations of men and women. The Church survives in spite of the humans who run it and it is that survival that gives the Church its mantle of invincibility.

The Church is the structure that has survived the collapse of the Roman Empire and the blood of its martyrs is seen in all parts of the world—even today. No human force could extinguish its fire and the strength of the institutions has given strength to even the most frail of us. A pastor once told me that if it God ordains something, it will survive. If not, it will die. Maybe that is the secret of the Catholic Church. And it is that secret that still ensnares even the weakest of us all.

4

The Christian Century

Here is a thought; the 21st century may be The Christian Century. Christianity is booming throughout the world and most of us in North America don't' know that or see it happening. Why are we ignorant of this trend? The reason is simple. First of all, throughout the Western world, Christianity is on the wane. In Europe, the Christian faith has given way to a secular faith and most churches are empty on a Sunday morning. Only in America is Christianity continuing to grow and this is due to immigration and faster birthrates than seen in Europe.

The center of the Christian world is now moving south to Africa and South America. In Nigeria, there are more practicing Anglicans than in England and Uganda is catching up as well. The Philippines have more baptisms per year than France, Spain, Italy and Poland combined. Not only that but there could be a theological schism developing between the new Christians in developing countries and their counterparts in the West, and Christianity is faring very well in the competition for the souls of the world's poor against Islam.

In 1900, Africa had only 10 million Christians, who represented about 9% of its population and today. Today nearly half of all Africans profess their faith in Jesus Christ. Latin America is practically all Christian and even in Asia, there are over 300 million practicing Christians. The growth of the Church in the developing nations is phenomenal and Professor Phillip Jenkins wrote, "in its variety and vitality, in its global reach, in its association with the world's fastest-growing societies…it is Christianity that will leave the deepest mark on the twenty-first century," The largest population of Christians now live in Africa and Latin America.

This boom will redefine the regions, politics and Christian theology. Within the Church, the more secular West is pushing for greater reform in its churches whereas the Christians of the Southern Hemisphere are requesting a return to a more traditional Catholic Church or are flocking to the evangelical version of

Christianity. At this point, Europe and America control the leadership of the major denominations but soon many in the developing world will challenge their leadership.

The changes in the South are operating contrary to those in the North where theology is moving from the more orthodox Christianity. Pentecostal and evangelical movements dominate the Protestant movements, and Roman Catholics are leaning toward a more orthodox bent. For many in North America and Europe, these beliefs border on reactionary. Many believers in the Southern Hemisphere look to spiritual revelation, exorcising demonic forces and are creating a new version of early Christianity.

As many of these countries move toward democracy, the newfound Christian faith is going to play a key role in the nature of these nations. In Africa and Asia, Church leaders stand for the Christian principles of justice and morality. During the 1980's, it was the Catholic Church and its leader that kept alive the hope of democracy under the nose of the Marxist regime in Nicaragua. In South Africa, the church played a key role in ending apartheid.

The real problem will be the direct competition with the growth of Islam for souls of the common person. We are seeing such conflicts in Sudan, Nigeria, and Indonesia. In Sudan, Christians are persecuted and occasionally enslaved by the government. It is estimated that Muslims in the North have killed two million Christians and animists in an attempt to Islamize the entire country.

While some predict a split between the Church in the Southern Hemisphere and in the North, others see a more ominous threat as Islam and Christianity veer toward a collision course for converts and influence in the developing countries. Crusades and jihad may yet bring ruin to various developing countries. In Nigeria, this conflict has the potential of spilling into the streets where Christians and Muslims are almost equal in population. Some in the Islamic community are pushing for the imposition of strict Islamic rules that could preclude the open practice of Christianity. An Islamic court recently sentenced to be stoned to death a 30-year-old pregnant woman for premarital sex, and similar attempts to impose an Islamic vision of society upon whole nations goes on throughout the Middle East and Africa. Christianity and Islam have the same root through Abraham and the result has been great civilizations. For the Christian, all persons stand equal before the eyes of God. Such equality can secure peace, freedom and representative government that protects the rights of all. As Christian influence grows in the developing nations, new civilizations may yet grow as these nations go from developing to being developed.

BOOK V

A Few More Thoughts

Editor's note: *Here are some random thoughts from Immigration policies to Pat Buchanan. I even tackle pop artists Alanis Morrisette and Avril Lavigne.*

1

Immigration Policies

Within the conservative and libertarian ranks, there is heated debate going on dealing with immigration. Over the years, scholars such as John Miller and Peter Brimelow have discussed what needs to be done or not done.

Immigration bans are standard operating procedure over much of the world., Brimelow points out that in Japan and India, immigration is virtually unheard of. In America, successive and overlapping cycles of immigration and nativism created policies ranging from virtual exclusion to periods of intense ethnic readjustment. Contemporary anti-immigration is found on all sides of the American political spectrum. Institutions as diverse as FAIR and the National Review have recently favored restrictions.

Let me state my own bias up front. I believe that access to American citizenship is one of the basic institutional freedoms, which distinguish and adorn American nationhood. Immigration like emigration is an emblem of liberty. That said, the critics of immigration make points, which must be taken seriously. Part of the popular revolt against immigration results from natural strains associated with the assimilation of new immigrants into the national culture. Part of the recent strain represents "transferences" of tensions created by the liberal social welfare state, visited gratuitously upon the heads of our most recent residents and citizens.

Only in the decade of 1900–1910 did America absorb a number of immigrants greater than in the decades of the 1980's. The proportion of arriving immigrants to residents—3.1 per 1000 in the 1980's—is lower than during any decade between 1830 and 1930.

Policy exacerbates tensions. According to a survey conducted by Stephen Moore and John Miller, close to 40 percent of Hispanic and Asian immigrants speak

English poorly nor not at all. Language is part of what sustains and unifies our culture. Bilingual education in public schools creates state-sanctioned balkanization and pro immigration spokesman Ben Wattenburg contends that proficiency in English ought to be a condition of citizenship. On this point, he is right.

Much of the debate on the merits of continued immigration boils down to economics. Peter Brimelow and others contend that immigrants are a net burden on the nation, based on a study done by economists Donald Huddle and George Borjas. Their study attempted to prove that immigrants cost more in taxes than they generated. There are several flaws to this rationale. Why single out immigrant groups for tax cost analyses? Why not the elderly? Why not students or members of the armed forces? Farmers? If what is being conveyed is that certain segments of the immigrant population are statistically prone to welfare dependency, why not clearly differentiate the economic impact of those particular group? Do all Americans currently cost more in public expenditures than they generate in taxes? Do we not see that in the deficits?

What are the anti-immigrants really condemning? Is it immigration, the deficit, or the welfare state? The "cost to taxpayers" could be eliminated by a reversion to the social welfare polices of earlier decades. And Peter Brimelow admits that the net economic effect of immigration, plus or minus, is in fact economically negligible.

George Borjas, anti-immigration proponent, echoed these sentiments. A few years ago, Dr. Borjas wrote, "Immigration has two distinct consequences. The size of the economic pie increases. And a redistribution of income is induced, from native workers who compete with immigrant labor to those who use immigrant labor." With these words, Dr. Borjas ended one phase of the battle over immigration. In a society where a deficit is an economic fact and has been for most of the past four decades, Americans in general cost more in public expenditures than they generate in taxes.

No longer do we hear that new residents don't pay their weight. The debate has shifted to a more conventional left wing theme: that immigrants cause income redistribution. "The debate over immigration policy," writes Dr. Borjas, "is not over whether the entire country is better off by immigration—it is over how the economic pie is sliced up."

Borjas' theory works this way: while immigration increases the overall economy, the major winners are the employers who pocket the excessive profits, while the workers see their income decline due to wage competition with immigrants. Even stout defenders of free markets such as the conservative National Review have fallen for this. In an editorial in the mid 90's, the NR staff wrote, "the effect upon America's exquisitely vulnerable blacks of the influx accidentally triggered by the Immigration Act is never discussed. Yet post-1965 immigrants and their descendants now outnumber blacks, whose progress has indeed simultaneously and suspiciously stalled."

At the time this was written, it was as black income was (is still) going up and the black-white education gap narrowed. These arguments mirror those of Pat Buchanan against free trade—that income is redistributed away from the poor and the middle class and toward the rich. This is a curious defense from defenders of the free markets. If economic freedom rationalizes production, why would it not rationalize labor? Karl Marx presented the only comprehensive counter theory: that the price of labor would fall not merely to its value, but to its replacement cost: slightly below subsistence. Then Marxism ran into history. The productive value of labor in capitalist nations created the highest standards of living for ordinary workingmen in recorded history. This happened because capitalists valued labor by the same standard that they valued other factors of production.

If government must "protect" wages through immigration restriction, why not protect wages directly, through minimum wage laws? If employers must pay labor more than it is worth, shouldn't government protect the price at which the fruit of such labor comes to market? Translating the immigration controversy into one of wealth redistribution is thus a dangerous path for conservatives: it plays to class envy, which threatens capitalist institutions. If one needs a few extra votes, just attack employers as greedy, or immigrants as predatory—and you can throw in that English Catholics are cliquish.

The strongest case for anti-immigration is cultural. Immigration has become the protective cover for a fashionable multi-culturalism that is more an anti-American demonstration than a celebration of diversity. This is more an agenda of the left than of the immigrants themselves. Former HHS secretary Donna Shalala stated, "I don't identify with the Pilgrims on a personal level," she was parroting the party line of America's leftist intelligentsia. Our strength lies in our Anglo-Saxon cultural institutions including private property rights, representative elections, and trial-by-jury endorsed by intelligent pro-immigrationists such as Joel Kotkin. "America," he wrote, "is an exceptional country with an exceptional kind of history…all made possible by Anglo-Saxon rules of law, fair play and due process. Without those, you can't have a multiracial society. No matter who comes or what happens, we have to hold onto this fundamentally Anglo-Saxon culture…Our biggest threat comes from small groups of activists who want to institutionalize racial, ethnic and linguistic communities in order to advance their own interests." Immigration without assimilation is indeed national suicide.

2

A Little Pop

A few year backs, Canadian Alanis Morrisette made it big with her album, "Jagged Little Pill" and at the age of 21, she became a star, a rock star. Morrisette successfully changed her image from the cutesy pop Brittany Spear teenage idol to hard edge female with angst. Her anger hit upon a central theme—men can be assholes. The latest Canadian import is Avril Lavigne. Lavigne sings pop, plays guitar, keeps her clothes on and like a Peter Townsend clone, smashes her guitar in a car window at the end of an MTV video. She is merely a rock and roller, a teen version of 80's Joan Jett—only without the leather.

Morrisette's first big hit, "You Oughta to Know" details the modern woman problem, being jilted by a man after being told it was forever. She sings, "You're still alive, and I'm here, to remind you of the mess you left behind when you went away." She reminds her former lover how she went down on him in a "movie theater" and wonders if his ex-boyfriend new lover scratches his back and shows passion in lovemaking. Lavigne, sings of teenage boys who travel by skateboards and who play the preppy scene. Morrisette talks of young adult relationships going sour, and Lavigne just talks of teenage boys who grow up to become MTV stars.

In Lavigne's world, his dream girl rejects "Sk8er Boi" because he is not preppy enough or cool. In the end, he becomes a rock star and finds a new love as the girl now realizes what she lost. Lavigne's song "Complicated" tells of the frustration when boys "have to go and make things so complicated...acting like you're somebody else makes me frustrated...." Lavigne merely rebels against boys trying to be who they are not.

Morrisette's first album details the little quirks of life, the man who flies for the first time and dies in a plane crash or the woman who sees the man of her life, only to find that he is married. All the paradox that makes up life becomes the subject of her songs co-written by Russ Ballard. (Speaking of Mr. Ballard, he was about to receive a commendation from the Mississippi legislature as a native son making it big before someone in the legislature actually read the lyrics of "You Oughta to Know." Somehow, a song about blowjobs in movie theaters and the occasional use of the f**k word did not seem quite, Mississippi like.)

In 1996, Morrisette made angst cool and talked a language that most young women understood. When I was in college, I remembered talking to a woman who had just been rejected by a man she cared for. As she told, "I gave him everything, I mean everything and what did I get? A fucking broken heart." The modern problem of the modern woman as the sexual revolution leaves its own scar. Lack of commitment plagues modern lovers. What Morrisette did was to remind us that there is a place for old-fashioned love, in which forever is not just a word. As she scoffs about her ex lover's new friend, "I'm sure she'll make an excellent mother." Somehow, boring girls are forever and women like Alanis appear vulnerable and expendable. Nearly 40 percent of women at many universities have a singles "hook ups", a euphemism for sexual contacts from oral sex and beyond. Lifetime promises translate into one nightstands or short-term affairs. The Morrisette of 1996 hit a nerve that translated into millions of CDs sold and it did not hurt that it had a nice beat.

Lavigne is pure pop but unlike Britney Spears, she rocks for her pop. Her music has a beat and it does not insinuate any sexual fantasy that does not exist. Spears played the tease but Lavigne does not tease, she just rocks. She is the cute girl next door, who just plays a guitar. (Okay, the girl next door rarely sticks her guitar in car windows but then, they do not dress like Britney Spears either.) Lavigne resembles the typical teenage girl more than Britney and her clones. Which is why she is hot. Of course, teenage girls grow up to become adult women and it is there that their music will and must change. That will be Lavigne's challenge, for rock tends to devour their young when they mature.

3

Patent Protection Under Siege

Right now, patent protections are under assault throughout the world. Under the Doha Declaration on Trade Related Aspects of Intellectual Property Rights (TRIPS), any government in developing nations can declare a public health emergency and bypass any patent for medical drugs or products—giving that nation the right either to import or locally manufacture generics. Goodbye patent protections for the pharmaceutical business.

The original goal of the Doha Declaration was to allow less expensive HIV drugs to reach Africa, which is presently suffering from an HIV epidemic and no means to treat the disease. Of course the problem is obvious to any one that studies economics, if companies patent rights are not protected then what are the incentives to continue research in HIV? With the recent belief that companies producing HIV drugs will see those patents stripped, research for HIV drugs have dropped by 33%. That means that there will be fewer new drugs and fewer future options as resistance develops to present therapies. Nor will this guarantee access or promote global health in the future, for to allow generic markets to grow at the expense of patented drugs is a lack of forethought. Never mind that drugs are still the smallest portion of global healthcare spending, the ability of the drug Industry to develop new therapies will be compromised with future patients as victims.

While a bigger and looser generic market would reduce costs short term, there is no guarantee that the poor will have access to these products. The Indian company Cipla sells anti-retroviral drugs to Kenya at $600 per year, which is actually more expensive than any drugs sold through the Accelerated Access Program. With the difficulty of monitoring HIV numbers, most African countries cannot manage the disease effectively. In South Africa, the government even refused to manufacture the deeply discounted combination drugs produced by a local firm under the voluntary license from Glaxo Smith Kline, the patent holders of these drugs. So many countries can't or will not manufacture these drugs. Therefore, availability is still restricted.

The real challenge for developing nations is not just getting the latest therapies in their hands but continuing the development of a steady stream of new medications. Without protection of intellectual property, private risk will not happen. Rarely mentioned is that the protection of patents stimulates technology transfer, which leads to increased investment and economic growth in developing countries. When intellectual property rights were strengthened in software, India became a leader of software development and both Brazil and China have seen more investment in their pharmaceutical sector following improvements in patent laws. We can see similar experiences in Africa.

Another problem is increased piracy. In countries where there are weak patent laws, piracy is a problem—whether it is jeans, software or pharmaceuticals. There are reports that many inexpensive drugs destined for Africa are now being diverted to Europe and being sold at premium prices. Many Africans are being denied these inexpensive drugs and many Africans are dying as a result. If Western governments concede the erosion of patent protection, this problem will only worsen. We will see more piracy of pharmaceuticals or diversion of pharmaceuticals to the more developed countries.

Of course, the reason that there is limited access to HIV drugs is not patents but lack of profit opportunities as much as anything. Nor is the production of HIV drugs in a poor country a guarantee that the poor will benefit. In India, HIV is growing at a rapid rate despite the presence of hundreds of generic drug firms and weak patent protection. The poor have access to inexpensive HIV drugs throughout India, and yet many do not take advantage of the treatments. This only shows that destroying patents of drugs and unleashing hosts of generic competition will not slow down the HIV epidemic.

Many activists pushing these ideas make no bones that their real goal is to destroy the patent system for the pharmaceutical business, period. Activists such as James Love of the Consumer Technology Project admit that they would like to see a relaxation of patents on any drugs manufactured for diseases such as AIDS, malaria, and tuberculosis. They would like to see the elimination of patents, worldwide. The ultimate goal is to destroy the private pharmaceutical industry and it does not matter who dies as a result. Future patients may be thanking activists such as James Love for the lack of new and innovative treatment for diseases.

Of course, the lack of patent protection extended to pharmaceuticals can easily be expanded to other industries. If we do not protect patents in the pharmaceuticals business, we will not defend them in other industries as well. Without patent protections, a market economy will have a hard time existing and innovating. Intellectual property rights are essential to economic development throughout the world. To defend intellectual property rights is to protect the entrepreneur whether they exist here in the United States or abroad.

4

Buchanan—A Man Yelling Stop

For a few brief moments, I joined the Buchanan brigade in 1992 when I voted for him in the Kansas primary. For me, it was a protest vote against Bush's failure to adhere to supply side economics. Today, I can say that I should have voted for Bush.

In 1996, during the South Carolina primary, Pat Buchanan made protectionism his centerpiece against Bob Dole. For many years, the textile industry fought for protectionism against foreign competitors and the textile manufacturers provided key backing to Buchanan's efforts—allowing Mr. Buchanan to elevate this issue front and center. What Buchanan missed was that South Carolina was no longer just an agricultural and textile state. In Greenville, there was a BMW plant, and during the first half of the 1990's, state exports abroad increased 68%. The bottom line, foreign trade and foreign investments were creating jobs and this helped provide a strong pro-trade countercurrent against protectionist fever. Dole swept the primary and the Buchanan candidacy pretty much ended. Whatever presidential aspirations Buchanan had, died at that moment.

Pat Buchanan, the solid conservative representative, learned politics at the knee of Richard Nixon, one of the least principled Republicans. Pat Buchanan, like Richard Nixon, considered the Goldwater campaign a debacle and as author Richard Nadler wrote about Buchanan, "Buchanan's blood may have been mujahadeen. His bones were pure establishment." When Goldwater made his famous acceptance speech in San Francisco Cow Palace declaring that extremism in the defense of freedom was no vice, Buchanan considered the campaign over. Thirty years later, Buchanan still felt that Goldwater should have done more to unite the party and that the speech was an unmitigated disaster. If anything else, Buchanan learned that conservatives without allies lose elections.

After a stint on the editorial staff of the St. Louis Globe, Buchanan went to work for Richard Nixon. Nixon was a brilliant politician but could be devoid of principle when it suited him. In 1966, Nixon set the ground for his comeback by working for many GOP candidates in a year they made substantial gains, and in 1968, he captured the GOP nomination.

Buchanan served in the Nixon White House as Special Consultant to the President and from there; he helped with speechwriting, briefing papers and correspondence. Along with Howard Phillips, he also served as Nixon's liaison to the conservative movement. (Phillips, like Buchanan, would leave the Republican Party. Both men would adopt similar positions in opposing the mainstream conservative movements of the 90's.) One of Buchanan's key jobs was keeping conservative activists on board when John Ashbrook challenged Nixon in the early 1972 primaries. In 1973, Buchanan wrote *The New Majority*, which celebrated Nixon's accomplishment in leading the Republicans back from the electoral brink in 1964 to challenging the Democrats as the majority party. He lauded Nixon's appointees to the Supreme Court including Harry Blackmun, who authored *Roe v. Wade* and *Doe v. Bolton*, which made abortion on demand a reality. Buchanan even supported Nixon's price and control policies. Contrast this with Phil Gramm, who as a college professor was writing tomes against price controls and Bob Dole, who was opposing abortion on demand. Buchanan praised the Nixon policies that gave America both. Within two years, Buchanan would repudiate his adoration of Nixon when the final results of Nixon's policy failures became obvious.

Buchanan observed that the conservative movement could count on only 25% of the population and future conservative Presidents would need to break the Democratic hold of the solid South and entice millions of Democrats to defect.

George Wallace, running as an Independent, took 46 electoral votes and close to 14% of the vote in the 1968 Presidential election and was the leading vote getter in the 1972 Democratic primaries before his candidacy was cut short by a bullet from an attempted assassination. After George Wallace could no longer campaign, the McGovern left wing rebellion took hold of the Democratic Party and this enabled Nixon to peel off a large contingent of Democratic voters. Watergate delayed the new alliance of blue-collar Democrats, southerners and the GOP.

Social issues such as abortion and racial quota would prove to be wedge issues that enticed many Democrats to cross over to vote Republican. In his essay, *Con-*

servative votes, Liberal Victories, Buchanan offered his form of apology for Nixon's polices and became a leading spokesperson for the conservative movement. Buchanan targeted the dependency that many Americans had on government and diagnosed quickly the problem—as long as Americans draw a significant portion of their income from government, there could be no support for limited government. As Buchanan was railing from the right on the problems of big government, a small group of intellectuals were leading a counterrevolution against Keynesian economics. Supply side economics was being developed but Buchanan did not jump on the supply side bandwagon. He wrote, "Battling recession with tax cuts and social spending is more pleasant and profitable at election time than fighting inflation." He sided with those within the Republican Party that what was needed was painful austerity to seek redemption from past fiscal sins. Ronald Reagan would reject the more pessimistic Republicans including Buchanan and campaigned on a platform of supply side policies. The policy worked and is now the competing conventional wisdom with Keynesian economics. Reagan policies slayed the dragon of inflation and ignited the greatest sustained peace-time economic expansion in American history.

In the 1970's, Buchanan decided that the Republican and the conservative movement needed to attract the working class and champion the producers and taxpayers of society. In American politics, each party walks into a general election with a base of 40% and the battleground is the middle. In the 70's, the Wallace voters occupied the middle, voters who were alienated middle or working class workers. For many of these voters, their home was the Democrat party but now they were rethinking their allegiances. Buchanan did not feel that appealing to conservative principles would work since conservative principles were not universally popular. Buchanan felt the conservative movement had to compromise to attract the blue-collar workers. He wrote in the mid-70s, "If to be fashionable we must devise affirmative action programs, let us discriminate in favor of the Democratic minorities we can win—conservative Jews, and Catholics in the Northeast and the working class and rural Protestants from the Border States and Deep South." He would employ the same strategy by supporting leftist economic policies such as protectionism combined with social conservativism in the 90's.

The problem with the Buchanan vision is that many of his economic allies do not share his social conservatism. His opposition to abortion is real and supported by many social conservatives but his opposition to the Gulf War and America's general involvement in foreign affairs has more appeal on the left than the right. His support for protectionism and his disdain for the business class in general also had more support on the left than the right. When he took over the Perot movement in the 2000 election, he basically ended the movement as a national movement. Many Perot supporters either voted Republican or did not vote at all and they were not pleased with his social conservative views. His left wing allies joined Ralph Nader or held their nose and voted Gore. He found himself alone with no supporters.

While the Reagan vision of supporting the GATT system and expanding NAFTA increased global freedom, the result of worldwide protectionism in the 20th century was fascism and war. In Buchanan's eyes, trade is war and everyone is exploiting America. The past twenty years have proven Buchanan wrong. Many were looking at Germany and Japan as models to follow in the 1980's. Japan today is mired in a ten—year recession and Germany is stumbling economically. Neither are models to follow today as America has easily outpaced both nations. As author Richard Nadler writes, "If free trade is an impediment, then the presence or absence of institutions which promote it—private property rights, civil libertarians, constitutional restraints on government—are geopolitically nugatory."

Buchanan's vision of economic autarky combined with social conservatism will fail. The Pro-life movement will only succeed in an alliance with free market advocates. This is an obvious since if the right to life or even be born is not protected, then all rights become suspect. Most pro-choice advocates are big government advocates. That is the flaw in the Buchanan's position. Today, Buchanan is now editing *The American Conservative* funded by Greek conservative Taki with the goal of redefining the conservative movement. At this moment, Buchanan stands alone as he did after the 2000 elections. A man on the fringe, yelling for history to stop as the rest of the movement passes him by.

5

Trade-American Style

It could be said that America was conceived in free trade. In the 18th century, the British pursued the economic theory of mercantilism, which controlled all aspect of trade within the Empire. Lord Sheffield explained the British position when he declared, "The only use and advantage of the American colonies or West Indies Islands is the monopoly of their consumption." The English parliament barred the import of American foodstuffs by high tariffs and legal prohibitions and set prices for the colonists. The major vehicle of free trade was smuggling, showing the corruption of the system. Trade wars between the European powers intensified in the latter half of the 18th century, some even escalating into actual combat.

After the French and Indian war, Parliament's interference with American commerce intensified through the passage of various legislations such as the Stamp Act of 1765. The revolutionary war had at its origin-protest against the prohibitions of free trade among the colonies and the British attempt to micromanage the colonies economic rights.

In the early years of the Republic, Adam Smith influenced the founding fathers and was a leading advocate of free trade. While Smith allowed for exceptions to free trade such as industry involved in national defense, and temporary subsidies for infant industries and temporary sanctions as retaliation, he made it very clear that the ideal economy included voluntary trade across national borders. As for his exception, the key word is *temporary* and Smith acknowledged that the retaliating nation would be hurt in the process. Both sides agreed with these exceptions to some degree and the Democrat-Republicans tended to believe in retaliation against adversaries who denied America commerce access to their markets.

Thomas Jefferson made the case for free trade when he wrote, "Instead of embarrassing commerce under the piles of regulating laws, duties and prohibitions, could it be relieved from all its shackles in all parts of the world. Could every country be employed in producing that which nature has best fitted it to produce, and each to be free to exchange with others mutual surpluses for mutual wants, the greatest mass possible would then be produced of those things which contribute to human life and human happiness." Thomas Jefferson only believed in trade sanctions as retaliation as tactics to *open up trade* and used these tactics against belligerents who attacked our commerce during the Napoleonic war. The Embargo Act and the Nonintercourse act were designed to punish the Europeans but the biggest victim was the Northeast United States. These areas suffered near depression conditions and what transpires was the first secession crisis in which a convention of Federalists considered nullification of federal law dealing with trade in 1814. This effort ended as the War of 1812 ended. These tactics failed to protect American commerce or enhance trade.

After the War of 1812, there was an agreement of the importance of American industry, the only question that remained—how to encourage the growth of American industry. Presidents Madison, Monroe and John Quincy Adams increased tariffs reversing past Democratic position and then for most of the period prior to the Civil War, the tariffs trended downward.

America was blessed with two very brilliant Secretaries of Treasury, Alexander Hamilton and Albert Gallatin at its inception. Both men believed in the superiority of the American worker but they had different ideas of how to develop that talent. Hamilton considered protectionism of infant American industry a temporary necessity whereas Gallatin was an ardent free trader. At this point in American history, tariffs were the main vehicle to raise funds for the government. The key issues were at what point was the tariff a fund raising mechanism and at what point did the tariff slip over to protectionism? In 1831, a Free Trade Convention was convened as a protest against the high tariffs in existence. Gallatin summarized the position of the convention when he wrote, "Moderate duties will also, as they always do, produce a greater proportionate revenue than when raised to an extravagant rate." Classical economics at work for even at the beginning of the American experience there was a clear understanding of tax policies. High rates could discourage commerce and be counterproductive. High tariffs did have the inverse effect of reducing revenues to the federal treasury as imports into the United States were reduced. The gamble by high tariff advocates was that local development would make up the difference of lost revenues.

Hamilton believed in government intervention in the economy but it was limited intervention. Hamilton realized that shifting capital from one sector to another would not increase the Nation's wealth. His goal was economic efficiency, for he believed that over time, as American industry grew—there would be competition. He never viewed protectionism as a jobs program. Of course in Hamilton's America, there were no labor unions, no income tax and no welfare state.

Henry Clay, like Hamilton, was a protectionist and he hoped to build America upon four pillars:

- A central Bank that would direct the nation's credit.

- A series of internal infrastructures such as canals and railroads.

- Redistribute the federal taxes back to the state for internal improvement.

- Protective tariffs to give America a competitive advantage.

Clay was the main antagonist in the various tariff debates and the debate centered on tariff rates. Most of the free traders considered rates of 25% or lower sufficient to raise revenues where as the Whigs and later Republicans would raise rates upward between 33% and 100%. Under the stewardship of Hamilton and Gallatin, the American debt was retired by the 1820s. From this point, the real debate was whether to lower tariff rates since the debt repayment was financed by tariffs. The free traders believed that since the federal government no longer was paying for debt servicing, the tariff rates could be lower. The protectionists felt that tariff rates should be higher to protect American Industry and pay for internal infrastructure developments.

Henry Clay was a pessimist whereas Hamilton was an optimist about the American worker. Clay saw victims in need of protection, a forerunner to the modern protectionist and welfare state advocate. Our overseas competitors were out to screw us, and everywhere in America there were Americans who needed aid. Trade was war and had to be fought as opposed to recognizing that trade was an important feature of a market economy. When the Whig party collapsed over slavery, many Whig politicians joined the Republican Party, including Abraham Lincoln. They brought their protectionist views into the neophyte party.

At the beginning of the Civil War, a big hike in tariff rates was passed and the tariff was not just designed to raise funds to fight the war but to protect Northern

Industry. In 1864, an even higher tariff was passed and this was to compensate businesses for various sales and income taxes passed during the war.

America grew into a world power during the second half of the 19th century but when you compare the average working man's condition, there is no doubt that the average worker prospered more over the past 50 years as opposed to the last 50 years of the 19th century. Whether it is wages or output per worker, the past fifty years have proven to be more productive. The GNP did average 4.3% growth per year in the last portion of the 19th century and that would not be reached until the 1960's. Massive Immigration was one key reason for this development.

The golden era of America's experiment with protectionism died during the Great Depression, when Herbert Hoover committed the double sin of increasing taxes in a recession while committing America to even higher tariff rates. What ensued was the Great Depression. In the 1930's, America had a trade surplus and had no economic growth. FDR did not reverse the tariff walls very much and kept in place high taxes and increased government spending. All this did was to delay economic recovery. Only after FDR began rearming America for World War II, did the American economy begin to boom.

The point here is simple, America rebelled against Britain due to Great Britain's control over American economy. The founding fathers understood Adam Smith, and even Alexander Hamilton, America's first protectionist, understood the limitation of protectionism. The tariff wall of the last half of the 19th century protected the monopolies that existed from competition and produced social strife. The only President in the last half of the 19th century who understood the problem of tariffs was Grover Cleveland, the last Jeffersonian Democrat elected President. Cleveland saw how high tariffs shifted resources of the economy to the more powerful while increasing the size of the federal government. He was unable to reduce the tariff significantly but he did help America recover from a serious depression in the middle of the 1890's's brought on in part by the McKinley tariffs passed before Cleveland took over the Presidency. The irony is that McKinley would be overwhelmingly elected in 1896 over William Jennings Bryan as the America economy was recovering. The depression of the mid 1890's did have a significant political impact. The populist movement took over the Democratic Party with the platform of inflating the currency to help the small farmers pay off their debts under more favorable conditions. Many populists were free traders but favored their own version of government intervention. The economic downturn destroyed what was left of the Jeffersonian small government Democrats. The combination of progressive Republicans and populist Democrats laid the groundwork for the welfare state. Those businesses that benefited from protectionism merely created new political enemies.

Today, the main protectionists come mostly from the left, with a few nationalist conservatives such as Pat Buchanan. For the left, the new autarky is based on an evil America exploiting world resources and third world worker. Tariffs are as much social taxation to punish global companies, as they are to supposedly help American workers. The Left understands that in a free trade era, those nations that over tax and over protect will be left behind in the global development sweepstakes. The goal is to reduce world trade and reduce the incentive of corporate America to move capital worldwide. In a world in which capital can move at the speed of light in cyberspace, modern day markets punish those countries that attempt to socialize their economies domestically. Free trade is the enemy of socialistic governments since companies and capital are no longer tied to the homeland. As for the conservative advocates of protectionism, it is a case of our competitors screwing America, and American workers losing jobs to third world cesspools. Of course, with that logic, Haiti should be one of the fastest growing countries in the world. What both the left and right advocates of protectionism fail to realize is that what makes a nation attractive to capital is stable money, a neutral judicial system, low taxes and a functioning market economy. Those nations without a judicial system to enforce contracts or patents do not receive significant investment. When many Americans are horrified about foreign investment in our country, many of these countries are equally horrified that *their capital is leaving their country for ours. They consider capital flight equally as horrifying as some of our protectionists considered foreign investment and foreign trade as evil!*

In the free trade era, many countries have been forced to reduce their top marginal rates, which means those countries see increased economic freedom. And many proponents of free trade just hate that. Economic freedom trumps socialism and that is what today's protectionist wants to protect. Socialism.

6

What Makes a Good Movie

My daughter published a piece on her website on what makes a good movie. She wrote, "A good story is real. Subtlety is good….A good story isn't how a perfect kingdom is run but how a King tries really hard to make sure his kingdom doesn't fall apart." My daughter relayed to me an Indian story about a king dressed up like a commoner to see what the common man and woman thought of his leadership. What he found was that they would never trust their king as long as their king's cheating wife still lived in the palace. What he learned surprised him. It was the surprise that makes this a good story for we find that the Kingdom was threatened from within.

Good stories begin with everyday people living in normal times forced to rise to an occasion that is seemingly beyond their control. As my daughter observed, "And for one moment they see beyond the everyday. They tell their story. They fall silent. The silence is important." The good storytellers do not explain beyond what is needed, and allow the audience to participate in their life and put themselves in the narrator's shoes.

These common individuals are people just doing their jobs. In *Gladiator*, Maximus was not interested in promotion or the offer of the Emperor Marcus Aurelius—all he wanted to do was go home. Maximus was willing to accept the offer of his Emperor only because it was job—a soldier's job is to obey his emperor. Maximus followed his penchant to follow duty and honor over mere glory. Maximus' stoicism was contrasted to the Emperor's son, who became the new Emperor after killing his father. Throughout the movie, Maximus's obedience to the virtue of the Old Rome of honor, duty and integrity is contrasted to a more frivolous boy, now the new emperor. That is why it was a good story and a good movie. We followed this man until his heroic end for we really cared what happened to him. We put ourselves in his shoes, following his every step and applauding his strength and character. The ending did not deviate from the story.

In the movie, *BraveHeart,* Mel Gibson's William Wallace was the common man forced to fight. All he wanted was to stay home, farm, and raise a family. He only fought and pillaged when the English tyrants took from him all that he treasured—his wife. His future died when she was executed and he first wanted vengeance and then freedom, for he realized that only when Scotland was freed from the English yoke could he and others like him live their lives as they saw fit. When he screamed "Freedom" at the end, we were screaming with him. King Edward finally saw that he could not win, for the death of Wallace created a martyr for the Scots to rally around. Even today, Wallace is a hero to the Scots and a reminder of a time when Scotland was independent of London.

A story that failed was *Minority Report.* During the movie, the Tom Cruise character was caught in a web that he helped to create and supported. In a society where even a thought could get you arrested, Tom Cruise found himself guilty of plotting the murder of a man he did not even know. The movie wondered how far would a Society go to maintain law and order? Do we really arrest a man for thinking about doing a crime or do we wait until the deed is done? Can an individual change his own future, or does what he think or plan actually happen? Tom Cruise found himself trying to change his own future while escaping from the local authorities. With the climatic end as he faced his own mentor, who was responsible for his fate—we were left with many questions. Then Spielberg ruined his movie with his concluding narrative. With a saccharin ending, Spielberg informed the audience that all will end well and that humankind learned all the right lessons. Up to that point, we were never sure what was learned. In real life, heroes do not always do what is right and we do not always learn the right lesson. In Orwell's *1984,* There was no happy ending as Winston Smith surrendered to Big Brother before the bullet entered his brain. Smith truly loved Big Brother at the moment of his death and he ceased to exist. In *Minority Report,* Cruise's mentor died at the end but his plan for the future of humankind was still in doubt. Uncertainty created unease about the future. At this point, the failure of the mentor's vision was obvious, but there was no guarantee that the lesson was learned. Instead Spielberg used the last five minutes to undermine what was a good story. He eliminated the uncertainty and in some way, went against the grain of his own movie.

The one movie that Spielberg succeeded with was Schindler's List. Oscar Schindler was a failed businessman who sees a golden opportunity. He could use cheap Polish Jewish workers to staff his factory. He convinced the German authority of his business savvy and immediately gets his own plant. What happens is that this failed businessman found success, using slave labor. As the war progresses, he started seeing his workers not as Jews but as humans. He also knew that his workers were doomed. His conscience began to distress his inner soul as he realized that he had to do something. So he began a list of "needed workers" and convinced the cruel German prison camp commandant to allow him to keep these workers under his purview. The story detailed his effort to save his workers and get them through the war unharmed. He became their Moses and in the end, he succeeded at great risk to himself. Initially, he made income that he could only dream of but he ended the war as he began-broke. The money that he initially made was used to ensure the survival of his Jewish workers. After the war, he continued his prewar business failure but he did win something bigger. His soul.

My daughter loved the book and the movie version of *Bridget Jones*. As she wrote, "She's not spectacularly smart. She's not royalty. She doesn't have millions of dollars or a perfect cellulite free ass. She's a spinster alcoholic who has to find a new job after an affair with her boss ends unpleasantly." Katharine found Bridget Jones someone she saw in every day life and could identify with. A good story combined with an everyday person struggling with everyday life.

Good Movies tend to sell themselves and bad movies just fade away very quickly. A good movie, like art, does not need to be explained. As my daughter discerned, "Picasso had put an essay next to Guernica saying "Look, this is what this is about." It would have stolen all the thunder and magic from the painting. And, just look at it, you know its about war. No one ever had to tell you that."

Orson Welles' *Citizen Kane* was the perfect story of what happened when avarice took over from idealism. Kane spent the early part of his life, fighting for what was right but he became corrupted by his own importance and gave up his political career for his mistress. While the movie implied that Kane's early childhood was responsible for his later actions, the reality was that his self-destructive behavior was his alone. Christian Kopff, the author of *The Devil Knows Latin*, wrote, "To give the Devil his due, I used to believe that no one who could rise to political prominence would be likely to risk it all for a tawdry love affair. History has taught me to appreciate Orson Welles' prescience." Bill Clinton, anyone? Welles risked everything on one affair and in the end he thought he was above rules—only to find that he was not. At the conclusion of his life, Kane became a bitter man and mere reactionary, not much different from the men he hated all his life. His last dying words went back to a time of innocence long since gone as he whispered Rosebud—the name of his sled as a young boy. As the sled burned in the fire, we saw the worth of Kane's life. A life of promise betrayed by Kane's ego. Welles' genius was not just being a good storyteller but his vision as a filmmaker. He set the stage for many filmmakers after this movie. His technique would be copied and aided in future storytelling. Welles was the young genius who would never climb this mountain again but then, most directors and producers would die for just one movie like *Citizen Kane.*

Space Odyssey was a masterpiece for it told a story of our possible origin. The combination of brilliant filmmaking that was ahead of its time and the story of man's dependence upon technology were told beautifully. When the computer Hal rebelled against the crew and sabotaged the mission, we cringed at the helplessness of the crew, as they had to go it alone millions of miles from home. The concluding scene left much to discuss and discern. We were left with questions that could not be easily answered. Man's origin was a mystery to the filmmaker and to us in real life. The search for who we are is man's eternal quest and *Space Odyssey* shows that search skillfully.

I must admit that I am a big Indiana Jones fan, and the Jones Trilogy represented the best of action features. We were presented with a college professor, who was not perfect and occasionally bent a few rules for his profession. Indiana Jones finds himself in many adventures but the first one, *Raiders of the Lost Ark,* set the tone as we are treated to one thrill ride after another. What was important is the message that even Jones failed to grasp until the bitter end, there are some things better left untouched. As one of Jones' colleagues reminds him, man was not meant to discover the ark. Jesus reminds us in the gospel, "Render the things that are God's unto God" and the ark was that one item. When Jones asked the government agents that hired him at the end of the movie about the fate of the ark, we see the absurdity of government bureaucrats as they put the Ark in a storage unit somewhere in Washington D.C.; hidden away from the world—forever lost. In the final movie, *Indiana Jones and the Holy Grail,* Indiana Jones was forced to give up the grail to save his life. Again the message of the ark held for the Holy Grail as well. There are some things that man was not meant to have. The ark had unspeakable power, and the Holy Grail gave the gift of eternal life. But the lesson was that man was incapable of handling the power of the ark, and that no man was meant to live forever on this earth.

Casablanca was one of those classic movies that stay with you, even today. The multiple layers of suspense, combined with great dialogue, suck you in. You can't escape as you really learn to care about the characters including the corrupt police chief. The main character, Rick Blaine, was a tired and cynical club owner, pretending to be oblivious to the world around. The world was engulfed in war but he created his own island at Rick's, his nightclub. As the movie unfolds, Blaine regains his idealism and makes the supreme sacrifice as he sends Ingrid, the girl of his life, on the plane with her husband. Bogart's last speech was masterfully delivered as he sent Ingrid way but as Claude Rains told Bogie, "She did not believe you." And we know that this was true. Of course, it doesn't hurt to have Nazis as the bad guys.

Another movie that I enjoyed was *Moulin Rouge,* which was criticized for being too slick for its own good. But as my daughter reminded me, "Moulin Rouge: Clever. Beautiful cut. Spectacular color, costumes aided by good dialogue. The icing on the cake? That both Nicole Kidman and Ewan McGregor are believable in their roles." To me, it was a story of love gained and love lost. We saw the pain of McGregor's own words as he became a writer, but a writer of tragedy, his own. It has been said, "it is better to have loved and lost than never to have to have loved at all." Somehow, McGregor may find such sentiments ludicrous as he wallowed in his own pain. The death of Nicole Kidman's character ended both the innocence of the age as well as the dream of McGregor and his bohemian friends. Convinced that all you needed was love, reality intervened with death and poverty.

Then there was the Godfather, the classic gangster movie. The opening saga had Don Corelone handing out favors at his son's wedding. What we saw was a clash of cultures as the Italian immigrant, Amerigo Bonasera asked Corelone to seek revenge for his daughter's beating at the hands of a powerful WASP. Corelone gave Bonasera a lecture on how he should have stood with the family and how in the past, Bonasera showed him no respect. Before this incident, Bonasera turned his back on his Italian heritage to become Americanized. Now he sought justice through the Mafia, rejecting the American judicial system. At the end of their discussion, Don Corelone reminded Bonasera that as a price for helping him, "Some day, and that day may never come, I will ask you for a favor." In the first movie, clients kissed the ring of the new Godfather, Michael Corelone as if he was a Roman Emperor. The contrast with ancient Italian history with the present America was unmistakable. In the second *Godfather* movie, Tom Hagan persuaded Pentagneli to commit suicide based on a story of ancient Rome and Pentagneli's suicide will spare his family. The Mafia operated as an underground miniature Roman Empire in contrast to the more materialistic American culture. What we see in the first movie and even in portions of the second, the Mafia with all its violence and illegality was not much different from the legal world outside. For the Mafia leaders, they considered themselves as legitimate as their legal counterparts and felt they were providing a service demanded by the population as whole.

Michael Corelone began the movie trying to avoid his family business and attempted to become Americanized. He fought in the war, he married a Wasp and now he was ready to set his own life outside the family business. Instead, as he said in the *Godfather III,* "I just keep getting sucked in." His life and rise to power was contrasted to his father. Don Corelone succeeded because of his loyalty to family and seeking revenge on his enemies and his son moved away from this precept and adopted a more monetary basis for power. For Michael, his family business was no different than other businesses and the criminality of it all did not bother him. For Don Corelone, he considered his family as his purview and he did what he could to keep it together and underneath his criminal mentality, his love for family was obvious. Michael's family collapsed as his wife left him and he had his older brother killed. For Michael, power destroyed all. While many criticized the original movie as glorifying the mob, by the time Michael took over the family business, we were cured of any illusions about the Mafia. Michael's actions took care of that as power corrupted him and destroyed his soul. The man who wanted to be more American, turned his back on what he considered important in the beginning to build a power based on fear and money.

A drama student wrote me about what she calls the concept in theater—the suspension of disbelief. The members of the audience accept the parameters of a story only if they accept the characters. You must be able to relate to the characters. *The Lord of the Rings* is one such story. In the opening scene, we see the happiness of the Hobbits village. It is here that Gandalf educates the Hobbit Frodo on duty and honor, for thrust upon Frodo's shoulders is the fate of mankind. He is to take the ring to Moldar to have destroyed. The ring corrupts all who hold it and is the key to stopping the evil that has been set upon the world.

The Lord of the Rings, written in the aftermath of World War II, explored individuals' responses in the midst of a clash of cultures and civilizations. What is at stake was the enslavement of all of Middle Earth in the hands of the Dark Lord Sauron. What was required was a coalition that must face the threat of Sauron that endangered them all.

Of course there were those who only sought neutrality in the upcoming struggle, hoping that the coming war will bypass them. Good Wizard Gandalf and Aragorn must begin the process of convincing all that what was at stake was nothing short of civilization's survival.

When Frodo felt drained from his mission, Gandalf reminded the little Hobbit that he would find the strength to continue, for the survival of all mankind rested upon his shoulders. Gandalf told Frodo, "All we have is to decide what to do with the time that is given us." At the end of the second movie, we are treated to one of the greatest battle scenes ever filmed. The 10,000 black-armored Orcs march on Helm's Deep in the darkness and rain of night. During the struggle that occurs, we are given a look at the children and women hiding in the caves and their grave looks give it all away. Their men are dying so that they may live and defeat means their demise as well. No man or child was spared from fighting and the victory of the Orc would mean the end of what was Rohan.

Treebeard and his companions decided at first that they would not participate but like the others in the film, the coming destruction sucked them in. They came to the realization that their forest was not immune to the upcoming slaughter and they fought, for they would die no matter what. Their attack upon Isengard corresponded with the attack on Helms Deep. J.R.R. Tolkien wrote this as an allegory of the world past and the world to come. For, he saw evil incarnate in Hitler, and then in Stalin in the post war era. For Tolkien, evil existed and was real. We don't really believe in true evil but it existed. In the Middle Earth, the peace was shattered by evil that was not at first really understood.

In Tolkien's world, the common soldier was a farmer not much different than Frodo or members of the upper class like Aragon. World War II was won on the back of the common man's sacrifice. In the *Lord of the Rings*, we see bravery in even the smallest, and in crisis there is a reserve of courage in all who struggled against Lord Sauron. So too, it was in real life. The Lord of the Rings was a great movie, because we see ourselves in this mythical world. The characters may be imaginary but they resemble real people that we know and see everyday in our lives. The message of the movie was that the fate of Middle Earth was in the hands of all from the little Hobbit to the immortal elves. The fate of all was entangled and no one could escape from doing their duty.

The good movies allow us the luxury of being entertained and educated. The good storyteller amuses us, humors us, and shocks us. But he leaves us wanting more and for me, a good movie is one that I can see over and over. A good movie has enough visual stimulation to get your mind involved. As your mind seeps deeper into the visual image upon the screen, the eternal truths that are part of every storyteller from the early cave men seep in. You are hooked.

7

Gods And Generals

Gods and Generals is one of those films that manage to get beyond the clichés to attempt to answer the big question: how can good men fight and die for a cause as odorous as slavery? Ron Maxwell's Civil War epic has been savaged by the critics, but only because too many critics view this movie in a 21st century prism. Some even viewed this as an apologia for the Confederacy, but it is not that at all. This is the prequel to Maxwell's *Gettysburg*, which was told mostly from a Northern point of view. This movie delves into the mindset of Robert E. Lee and his right hand man, Thomas "Stonewall" Jackson. To understand these men, you have to understand the debate about what it meant to be an American in the mid 19th century.

Was the Union one and indivisible, or a collection of states whose rights include secession? In the early 19th century, the debate over the right of a state to secede from the Union resounded from all sections of the country. After the War of 1812, many Northern States considered leaving the Union and then when the debate over slavery became heated, the South reserved the right to leave the Union if their way of life was threatened. Throughout the first half of that century, the issue of the right of a state to secede was not settled. For a people who never traveled far—the concept of the home state was as important as being part of the United States. Many Georgians or Virginians viewed themselves as Virginians or Georgians first and Americans second. So defense of one's homeland meant to defend their home literally. Certainly *Gods and Generals* do not put slavery front and center but it does not need to. Maxwell already assumes that the audience is opposed to slavery and what reference there is—is anti-slavery.

Robert E. Lee was given the chance to lead the Union Army, which he turned down. For Lee, his duty was to Virginia first and was appalled by Lincoln's call up of 75,000 volunteers to put down "the rebellion." While Lee did not initially support secession, he eventually stayed with his fellow Virginians to defend his homeland. Stonewall Jackson is Maxwell's main spokesperson for the South in this film. Jackson is a complicated man, a man who was a devout believer but yet capable of cruelty. To him, this was a war to the death and no quarter would be accepted. When he first meets JEB Stuart, he tells Stuart that there is no quarter in the upcoming war. When he debates with his aide on the fate of a deserter, he reminds his aide that if the South loses, they lose everything, whereas if the North loses, their soldiers go "back to their factories and their home, and enjoy their war profits." He even tells one General that he would just as soon not survive the war if the South loses.

Jackson is a Calvinist, who believes that all actions are preordained. When he leads his troops at the first battle of Bull Run, he serenely stands amidst the exploding cannon balls and bullets. When one of his aides asks how he can stand so calmly, he answers that it is faith that carries him. Jackson calls his men the "Army of the Lord" and his concept of God is an austere God, who has already cast his judgment, and we just merely watch His will be fulfilled. Jackson viewed slavery as ordained by God but if slavery ends, it will end at God's timing not at ours. Jackson viewed man's role in history as largely passive. It is not up to man to work out God's will but to accept it. As for his bravery, Jackson believed that his death was preordained and when his time came, it would come. This stoic attitude allowed him bravery under fire but it also allowed him to be cruel to his enemy. In Jackson's zealotry, the enemy must be crushed. Nowhere does Jackson ask God, if indeed the South's cause, is righteous. He just assumed that it was. His certainty is made clear when he debates with his aide, the coming execution of three deserters. His aide is not as certain and finds that maybe there should be a way out for these deserters—especially due to the fact these men are part of Jackson's "Stonewall" brigade, and were there with Jackson at the first Bull Run. For Jackson, there is no compromise and discipline is paramount. No exception can be made. Jackson is given a human dimension and we can sympathize with him, even if we do not agree.

Jackson's more austere God is contrasted to Union Colonel Joshua Chamberlain's God. Chamberlain, a philosophy professor, is a man trained in classical thinking. Before one battle, he tells his troops the story of Caesar crossing the Rubicon and concluded his speech, "Hail Caesar, we who are about to die, salute you." In another scene, he acknowledged that though slavery had always been with us, it still did not make it right. He found the irony in that his opponents claim to fight for their freedom while enslaving a portion of their own people. He was prepared to die to end this course and "free the Negro, then God's will be done." His God is a more forgiving God and man's role is not passive. If injustice exists, it must be undone and not wait until "God's Will be done." This film asks many interesting theological questions, which may be why this movie may be hard to sell in this more secular time. This is a clash of religious visions and many secular reviewers miss the debate that is going on. Is our life preordained and is there nothing we can do about God's Will? Or is free will a part of life and does this free will allow us to challenge the very injustice that exists within our midst?

It is on the question of slavery that Southern positions conflict. Jackson tells his cook that there are members of the general staff including Robert E. Lee as well as himself that wanted to recruit blacks into the army in exchange for their freedom. He added that this will help rebuild the South after the conflict but this strategy undermined the peculiar institution, which was the rationale of the southern society of that time. It also undermined one of the important reasons that many southern leaders committed themselves to this struggle. As for the African-Americans themselves, the two major black characters bond with their masters but yet it does not deter their desire to be free. As the female character, Martha, tells a Union general, "I was born a slave, and I want to die free." Even if these slaves love their masters, they still desire their freedom. They understand and see the oppression of their race.

This movie demonstrated the separation of a nation. In the beginning of the war, we see a friend of Jackson and Stonewall debate the upcoming war as the friend's son is signing up to fight with Jackson. As the friend tells Jackson, eventually slavery will end and the war will be a disaster for the South. Throughout America, this debate went on and the most dramatic example of this is when a Southern Irish brigade slaughters an advancing Northern Irish brigade at the battle of Fredericksburg. As one Irish soldier comments to Chamberlain, "I am fighting many of my friends I came over to America with. We escaped tyranny to fight each other in the land of the free." A confederate Irish officer weeps after the battle as he witnesses the many fallen Union Irish men dead on the field in front of him. One touching scene in which a Union soldier and a Confederate soldier exchange coffee and tobacco across a stream around Christmas time.

The battle scenes show the price that both armies paid for their side. For many Confederate soldiers, this was a defense of homeland for many of these soldiers were too poor to own slaves. For many northern soldiers, it was the Union they fought for and not necessarily to free the slaves—though that was the end result. As Colonel Chamberlain commented, the nation had to deal with the moral question of slavery. As the war progressed, slavery loomed as the main issue of the war and this ceased to be just a war to preserve the Union. Soldiers had to deal with harsh conditions throughout the war and for many soldiers, the price to be paid was high and in the end, worth the cost in blood. And the Union was preserved

8

Courtesan In America Today

"You went away to foreign peoples, and I stayed behind, the prey of that fire, which, without you, made my days black and sad; but as the hours progressed, little by little, I resolved to make a virtue of my need, and to make room in myself for other concerns. That was the true solution to my pain: in this way my mind discovered at last a cure for its deep and serious wounds; your departure for foreign lands mended the blow, although the scar mended the blow, although the scar could not be completely erased."
Veronica Franco, a 16th century Courtesan and poet.

Veronica Franco was a 16th century courtesan in Venice and a poet whose poetry described a more romantic view of love. Ms. Franco's life demonstrated both the advantage and problems of the courtesan. A courtesan provided companionship to her suitor from intellectual conversation to sex and in turn, the suitor helped the woman to fulfill her potential. Venetian businessman Domenico Venier was Franco's mentor and through his generosity, her poetry enthralled the world, even long after her death.

But the courtesan's relationship may prove problematic. When Venier died, Franco was left with little financial support and reportedly died in poverty. After a lifetime of being a lover for some of Venice's powerful men and establishing herself as a successful poet, she also had to fight off charges of witchcraft and a series of inquisitional trials. In the end, she would die a humiliated woman but today, we still have her words, which outlived her accusers.

Throughout history, courtesans have played roles behind the scenes of great men. Voltaire's mistress, Madame du Chatelet, translated Newton's *Principia* into French and King Henry II's courtesan, Diane de Poitiers, introduced the Renaissance into France. Courtesans were present in ancient Greece and were the noble line of geishas of Kyoto.

Evelyn Forsthye is bringing back the Courtesan tradition in 21st century America. What is the difference between a prostitute and a courtesan? Ms. Forsthye explained, "a prostitute is paid for sex. A courtesan is paid for her companionship as an erudite, engaging, sensual and beautiful woman." A beautiful woman, Evelyn is a woman of many interests and that is what makes her attractive to her gentlemen companions. As Evelyn told me, "If someone obviously isn't interested in talking to me about life, the universe, and the everything, then I don't think a date will work our for either of us."

Ms. Forsthye bristles at the suggestion that what she does is prostitution and added that not all of her dates end in sex. "People assume that I don't find my clientele attractive, so the payment is incentive to have sex," Evelyn told me, "I'll admit that when I started this work, I did think it would be like that, but it isn't…Yes, I have been with a companion, without the sex." For Evelyn's clients, it is the companionship that matters and she admits, "In fact some of these men I find so attractive, I think of it as being paid more to "go away" when our time is over rather than to stay!"

"A successful man is attractive, because he carries himself in such a way that bespeaks his confidence…Intelligence is extremely sexy. I have had the very best and most torrid romances with brilliant men," Evelyn commented, "So the sex is, if it happens, always voluntary on my part and has nothing to do with being paid." Evelyn Forsthye states that in any good date when the chemistry is right, "you feel compelled to consummate that."

Ms. Forsthye became a courtesan by evolution. "For a couple of years, I was involved with an illustrious physicist who was married. It didn't start out as a matter of compensation, but as things got more demanding of my time, he felt obliged to offer me money," Evelyn Forsthye said, "When his wife found out, he had to end things." Ms. Forsthye liked the arrangement and decided to see if other men would be interested in something similar. As she told me, "It turned out that there were men interested and the rest is history."

According to Ms. Forsthye, this is the dark ages of courtesanship. For many, being a courtesan is no different than prostitution but as she observed, "When someone has prostitution in mind, they think of sex. They think of raucous, instant gratification with no other interaction. A courtesan is closer to a girlfriend or wife than girlfriends or wives would like to believe." A courtesan provides companionship, conversation and passionate, voluptuous romance for short period like a weekend. For the man, he has a lovely companion with no strings attached. This relationship can last for a longer period. Evelyn Forsthye explains, "Many of my relationships are with wealthy men who are very busy, and just don't have time for a normal relationship. They can't meet the expectations a normal girlfriend or wife may demand of their time." For many men, it could be weeks before they are free to go out socially and it is simpler to compensate a courtesan. "I don't call them (Unless they want me to)," Evelyn continues, "I'll be there when it is convenient."

How particular can a courtesan be in selecting a companion? Ms. Forsthye relayed to me, "Among the inquiries, I tend to be bit picky." But as in other businesses, reputation helps to build one's resume. "I think it might be more accurate to say that they pick me," Evelyn told me, "Since there are plenty of other very beautiful women to pick from my rate range—they come to me because they are looking for the strong intellectual experience, as well."

Evelyn Forsthye is a liberated woman when it comes to sex and has "noticed a revival of fundamentalist Christian values that has resulted in a lot of cultural hostility towards sex." Evelyn Forsthye in some ways may sound like her fundamentalist Christian opponent when she observed, "Contrast this with the distasteful way that sex is portrayed on television. The result seems to be a massive confusion about what part sex should play in a person's life." Evelyn's observation is that sex is used as a political and social tool by mainstream commercial interests more "vigorously than any prostitute" would use sex.

Sex can be used in a subversive and manipulative way and this can be unhealthy. "For instance, the wife who won't have sex with her husband unless he performs other duties under God to service," Ms. Forsthye remarks, "Or the commercial that uses sexual innuendo to sell a health product on the vapid premise that it will increase your sexual appeal."

Evelyn is an atheist but her beliefs have nothing to do with her career choice. Her father was a Lutheran but not a "practicing one" and the only time that the family ever went to church was on special occasions. It was her study of science that made belief become irrelevant to her.

Evelyn is most interested in the serious side of life—science, history, politics and philosophy. These interests become obvious when one visits her website. Her daily diary carries her views on everything from Voltaire, modern day feminism to foreign affairs with a little levity thrown in. For those who are looking for tell all, Evelyn will disappoint. For those who are interested in an intellectual look at the world with a few unique twists, well this is the site for you. Ms. Forsthye shows the most interest in Science and philosophy in her readings, as her favorite authors include Karl Popper, Thomas Kuhn and Carl Sagan. She has studied the great philosophers such as Hobbes, Hum and Spinoza. The one individual who changed her life was Mark Lehner an archaeologist and expert on the Egyptians.

"Ever since I was a little girl, I've been fascinated by the Egyptian pyramids. Of course, the mysticism that surrounds them was compelling as was the richness of the culture," Evelyn said, "However, the more I read what archaeologists were writing about it, the more I realized that the pyramids aren't mystical at all. It turns out that they were built by the Egyptians, using some really innovative methods, and that's certainly fantastic, but not supernatural." By studying Mark Lehner's story about the Egyptians struggle to build the pyramids; she realized that human ingenuity created the pyramids. It was not aliens from space nor was it an easy task but one fraught with many failures before success was reached. Evelyn questioned many of her assumptions about mystical beliefs and as she stated, "Which immeasurably enriched my life and comprehension of the world I live."

Another aspect that changed was her political beliefs. She is now a libertarian but it was not always that way. "For a long time, I worked in science education as the chair and program director of several different non-profits, and to a limited extent I still do. Being exposed to the world of grant-money tends to focus a person's opinions in one discrete direction or another," Evelyn Forsthye explained, "Many of the people I worked with were socialists—even if they didn't realize it—and some were very liberal….Initially, I leaned in that direction, as well."

Her experiences with less than savory socialists as well as financial losses in her non-profit social organization changed her perspective. "In order to have philanthropy, you have to have a certain amount of wealth. So where does that wealth come from?" Ms. Forsthye asked rhetorically. Her answer was that wealth came from taxpayers and the entrepreneur.

And her pronouncement on foreign policy is hawkish. The woman is no shrinking violet and like many of us on the right, understands that peace begins in the Middle East when Saddam Hussein is six feet under. And the woman can discuss the flat tax proposal of Steve Forbes with the same aplomb that she can discuss Aristotle. A Renaissance woman.

Why be a libertarian? Evelyn answered, "Libertarians are the only party today that seems to have that which embodied most of my ideals…I'm conservative about the economy and foreign affairs. I am a social liberal.. the government has no business legislating my personal life." Nor does Evelyn have much use for many of today's feminists. But then, Evelyn Forsthye feels emancipated in her own for she has control of her life and whom she sees. Her affairs are arranged to her advantage and that of her lovers.

Throughout history, the Courtesan has been the mystery behind many great and powerful men. There are rules to be followed and to be a Courtesan, you have to both independent and in control of the situation. There are no pimps to gather clients or to share the wealth. The Courtesan has her foot in the door of the wealthy and to be a successful Courtesan, a woman must exhibit an entrepreneurial spirit to go with intelligence and an understanding of basic business. In other words, a capitalist.

"You went away to foreign peoples, and I stayed behind, the prey of that fire which, without you, made my days black and sad; but as the hours progressed, little by little, I resolved to make a virtue of my need, and to make room in myself for other concerns. This was the true solution to my pain: in this way my mind discovered at last a cure for its deep and serious wounds; your departure for foreign lands mended the blow, although the scar could not be completely erased." Veronica Franco

BOOK VI

Conservatism Revisited

Editor's note: Defining conservatism is not so simple. American conservatism seeks to conserve but yet it favors change. It does not seek revolution but it is okay with evolution. Conservatism does not oppose change but understands to change the future does not mean to undermine the past. This essay attempts to go beyond my own definition of conservatism that I established in the Introduction of my first book, Economics 101 and Other Thoughts. After the chapter, I introduce two outstanding women, who represent various aspects of conservatism. This piece profiles two conservative women. Michele Catalano is a New Yorker whereas Carol Golden lives in the middle of the fruited plain—Iowa. I communicated with Ms. Catalano via EMAIL and as for Mrs. Golden—she is my editor.

1

The Philosophy of Conservatism

"The liberty we prize is not America's gift to the world; it is God's gift to humanity."
George Bush, State of the Union 2003

These sentiments begin the process of defining the American conservative. We do not believe that the state or the nation is the highest authority but our freedom and liberty are gifts that are naturally endowed; not a gift merely bestowed upon us. President Bush's point is simple; we are all answerable to a higher authority. To be conceited in our own self is the beginning of hubris.

Christopher Hitchens, the British born leftist pundit, wrote, "When viewed from any objective standpoint to its immediate left, the American conservative movement manifests one distinct symptom of well-being. It is fairly conspicuously schismatic, and it possesses the confidence to rehearse its differences in public."

Hitchens concedes that today's political left is merely the status quo and as Hitchens observed, "American conservatives have won some deserved respect for their willingness to attack the status quo and for their ability to know a historical turning-point when they see one." From the American Revolution till modern times, American ideals are proven to be essentially conservative. Our founding fathers chose a Revolution to preserve and conserve what they believed was their right as Englishmen of their era. It was not a revolution to change mankind in contrast to most revolutions that followed. The French Revolution that would follow within a decade of our own went in a totally different revolutionary direction. Instead of preserving order, the French revolutionaries attempted to change the nature of men. As Alexander Hamilton would write in the Federalist Paper, "If men were angels" we would not need government." For our founding fathers, revolution was not to change man but to seek an ordered liberty to restrain the natural inclination of man. Our founding fathers were not believers in the perfectibility of man and founded a government that understood that. The French

153

revolutionaries believed in the perfectibility of man and that only with the right law and incentives, the new man could be created. Their revolution ended up with Napoleon, who in the end saw himself as the new emperor of Europe. So much for the new French man.

When author Roger Scruton in a Wall Street journal article attempted to answer the question, what did conservatives want to preserve, he answered, "Us...At the heart of every conservative endeavor is the effort to conserve a historically given community...He is the one who looks for the good in the institutions, customs and habits that he has inherited." Scruton continues by noting that conservatives are "suspicious of experiments and innovations that put loyalty at risk." For Scruton, conservatism is less a philosophy than temperament that emerges "naturally from the experience of society."

According to Scruton, conservatives love the free market not just because it works but also because it forces individuals to take responsibility for their own actions. American conservatives are not shy about defining its philosophy at an intellectual level and Scruton compares American conservatives with those in his native Great Britain, saying that "British conservatism has always been suspicious of ideas and the only great modern, conservative thinker in my country who has tried to disseminate his ideas through a journal—T.S. Eliot—was in fact an American.". Scruton views conservatism not just about profit but "about loss: It survives and flourishes because people are in the habit of mourning their losses, and resolving to safeguard against them."

American conservatives are not like European-style conservatives for American conservatives do not defend a hierarchy nor do the American conservative have a pessimistic view of humanity. We do not believe that men are angels but we do not necessarily believe that men are devils either. A conservative, American style, is really an old fashioned liberal. There was a time in American History that to be a liberal *was to be for less government, open trade and more freedom.* I reviewed a book on the life of Grover Cleveland, who best represented what liberalism used to be. He stood on the rampart against government spending, spent his presidency trying to *lower tariff barriers and reduce the tax burdens on Americans.* He was the last of the classic Jeffersonian liberals. As the 19th century came to a close, what was left of the Jeffersonian liberalism died with Grover Cleveland's political career.

In the 1950's, during the beginning of the Cold War, Bill Buckley redefined conservatism. Combining libertarian economic thoughts with social conservatism and adding the Anti-Communist factions, Buckley was able to fuse together a new conservative movement. Even today, the combination of this conservatism still exists. Buckley originally started his movement by yelling, "stop" to the progressive movement propelling through the 50's. American conservatism is not about stopping change, but allowing the individual to affect change as opposed to government. Conservatives are the biggest defenders of free markets, and free markets are about change. To stand for free market is to defend change on a daily basis for the consumer drives it. What conservatives' distrust is change instituted from above, from government.

William F. Buckley wrote recently, "Conservatives do not vest in the free market ontological authority. But we believe that the marketplace is the operative mechanism by which individual choice is transcribed." Individual choices matter. Buckley gives the example between Pepsi and Coca-Cola in which he discerns, "On such matters conservatives are nescient, never knowing which of the two is better, capable of knowing which is in greater demand."

Today, two out of every three jobs that existed a century ago, do not exist. Who would want to have manure scoopers to clean up after horses? That is one job we could live without. On the other hand, conservatives understand that society does need a glue to hold the center together. Respect for the rule of law, a common bond of morality and justice and finally, the need of religious practices are a necessity to a functioning democracy—if only to remind us that we are not gods and that our leaders, like ourselves answer to a higher authority. Conservatives accept the idea that government serves the people and was established to protect the rights of the individual. When government becomes too big, it becomes a threat to individual rights. Free markets bring both change and turmoil and this is seen in the debate over free trade and Globalization. Free trade is threatening because it undermines the status quo. Those who oppose Globalization are the ones who oppose potentially progressive changes. Democratic free market societies can, in the end, assimilate what comes before it. With the individual driving change, society can evolve naturally. Democratic market societies encourage evolution, not revolution.

Over the past five decades, conservatism has not always seen the truth for in the case of race relations, it failed. Many conservatives viewed states rights as more important than the old principles of classic liberalism that geared it base. Unfortunately, the principle of state rights meant supporting the right of local govern-ment to deny a significant portion of its population their basic rights which should have been incompatible with what modern day conservatism was and is all about.

Today, it is conservatism that is now standing on the rampart of the principle for a color—blind society. Through the support of welfare reform, educational choice and finally, the opening of economic opportunities for all, conservatives are now regaining the moral authority on the question of race and it is the left that supports the status quo that oppresses minorities in inferior schools and demands government dependency. It is the left that argues that race matters and equality before the law does not. It is the left that is becoming the new segrega-tionist.

The one area where conservativism believes in preservation is in the courts. Anto-nin Scalia described the present Supreme Court activity: "Day by day, case by case, the court is busy designing a Constitution for a country I do not recognize." The Courts have become an un-elected legislature, usurping in many areas what should be left to the individuals and their legislature. The left has used the courts as a vehicle for "permanent revolution." A conservative jurist believes that to interpret the Constitution is to discern the original intent of the founding father. The Constitution does have a vehicle for change by the electorate and certainly conservatives are not opposed to change. What they fear is a Court that is not answerable to the people instituting changes that are not consistent with our founding father and our traditions. Robert Bork declared, "Legal conservatism requires discriminating judgment about what law can accomplish and what it cannot. Poorly thought out legal innovations do great damage." This is evident in Roe vs. Wade and its follow up decision, Doe vs. Bolton. These two court deci-sions have produced the most permissive abortion laws in the world. The right to privacy in which the decision is based upon is not found in the Constitution and before 1973, local governments made their own decisions about abortion laws. In many states, abortion laws were being liberalized to allow more leeway between the mother and her physicians. Kansas and California led the way in the liberal-ization of abortion laws. Abortions were being allowed under certain conditions while acknowledging the rights of the mother, the unborn child, and the sensitiv-ity of the local population. What Roe Vs. Wade did was to overturn 50 state laws including the most liberal. What it attempted to do was to end the debate on the issue. Instead of allowing a compromise to be reached, it went beyond the Constitution and stated the opinion of nine men in black robes on a complicated issue that was best left in the hands of the people.

What would happen if Roe vs. Wade were overturned? Simple, the matter goes back to the state and somehow, the American people will decide for themselves how to deal with this issue. Abortions would still be allowed in most states but the right would be restricted, depending upon locality. The Courts are the final arbitrator of the Constitution meanings and when the Courts go beyond their responsibility, respect for law is eroded. Justices can't substitute their own vision of law. It is here that conservatives need to stand up and say, "Stop." Revolution can never be instituted from above without destroying the fabric of society. American conservatives understand that change must come from below and through consensus. The leftist activists on the Court have no faith in the people and no belief in the Constitution but only in their vision of a just society. Using the Court to institute revolutionary change from above, they have eroded the authority of the Courts.

Indian author Gurcharan Das once observed that democracy is best in the hands of modest men. Modesty is a virtue for it is in modesty that individuals understand that there are limits to government and limits to what the courts can accomplish. Why conservatives believe in limited government is simple. The ability of government to solve all problems is impossible, and government is but one actor in society. Within the whole of society, many players interact from local businesses and local churches to local communities. Society is made of many parts and government is the legal vehicle to ensure that justice is for all. It is the vehicle to protect our right, not to abuse them. Government protects the freedom to worship, to speak out, to work and establish business. The hallmark of a conservative is modesty.

2

A Tale of Two Conservative Women

Michele Catalano is part of a new revolution, the blodger revolution. Armed with a computer key and linked to cyberspace, Ms. Catalano lays waste to the prevailing wisdoms along with other online pundits. I first heard of Ms. Catalano from the website, *Instantpundits* designed by Glenn Reynolds. Reynolds' vision was to connect various writers and pundits via the Internet and debate the big issues. You can read all points of view from every angle and the debate is never boring.

Michele's *A Small Victory* website is one of the more lively sites, as she takes no prisoners with her acerbic wit and clear cut ideas—you know where she stands. Combining modern day cultural references to rock, detailing her family adventures and the latest take on the big issues of the day, Ms. Catalano digests the latest issues with a unique twist that goes beyond the normal punditry seen in the mainstream media.

Like any mother with a new teen, she wrote, "More fear inducing than it's something than. It's something that makes me cower in a corner, longing for the days of yore. Natalie has a boyfriend." The human side of Catalano comes through in her writing as we get to know her and her family. Michele writes that she is "40 chronological. That would be 20 mentally and 5 socially" and she brags about her 22 year old husband as she tell her readers, "eat your heart out, girls." She is proud of her children but complains that their choice in music is "crappy."

Like many conservatives, Michele believes that peace begins in the Middle East when Saddam is six feet under. In one compelling piece, Michele reminds her audience what has happened over the past 12 years before the present conflict from Saddam's defeat in the first gulf war to his present shenanigans, by showing pictures of her 13 year old from one year of age to her present thirteen years. The point is that twelve years of stiffing United Nations resolutions is twelve years too long and you get the message by simply looking at the two pictures of Michele's oldest daughter. Not exactly a rush to war. On March 6th, she writes, "Either shit or get off the pot. The options are pretty limited. Either we move in force and take Saddam out or we let the U.N. have their way and give Saddam infinity plus years to disarm." No straddling the fence.

Her take on environmentalist issues is very simple, "I drive an SUV. If you don't like that, well...fuck you." A hard nose capitalist, she tells of her basic reasons for reaching out with the website, "I pay for the hosting, I pay for the domain name. That makes it mine and it means I can do whatever I want with it."

While she maintains a free market approach to economics and hawkish appreciation on America's role in the world, she takes a libertarian position on social issues, being pro-choice and supportive of gay rights. As she tells her readers, "The only time I will delete a comment is if it is threatening to another commenter or if it can be deemed as outwardly racist, anti-Semitic or homophobic. If you want to post that kind of venom, get your own site and do it."

Michele is not a religious person, in fact she is an atheist, which would make her a minority among conservatives. If nothing else, this blodger is proof that conservatives don't march lockstep on every issue.

Whereas my knowledge of Ms. Catalano is through a few EMAILS and her website, Carol Golden is a close friend. I first met Mrs. Golden during the 1996 Iowa caucus when I was working for Phil Gramm and she was working for Buchanan. Born in the South, Mrs. Golden began her life as a Democrat. Her change to the Republican Party and the conservative movement was due to her pro-life position. "I always believed in pro-life and the liberals got more and more away from life values." Mrs. Golden said, "They also seemed to feel that women couldn't make it without someone to help them and that upset me." When Carol was growing into political maturity, the Democrat party had what was called, the "Scoop Jackson wing." This was made up of liberal Democrats who were hawks on defense issues and on social issues. She was a part of that wing of the party but felt that they were not able to accomplish their goals and whose voices were stifled at every turn. Thus, she made the switch to the Republican Party.

She began her journey to the Republican Party and true conservatism over a period of years. "I was a moderate conservative in 1983 when I switched my affiliations to the Republican Party. I am a real conservative now." Carol said, "I believe in the Constitution as our Founding Fathers intended it." Like the modern conservatives and libertarians, Carol believes that "every person has value and that no group should be discriminated against or given special rights over another....A true conservative does not look at race, religion, culture, gender and say that any of those needs special help"

The one thing that unites libertarians and conservatives is that it is the freedom of the individual that matters, and they do not identify themselves as part of specific groups. There was a time when Carol was a Democrat, that the political left and liberals believed in the worth of the individual and all were created equal. Today, it is the political left that plays identity politics.

While Michele takes a more social libertarian position on abortion, Golden is a leader in the pro-life movement. Carol's concern for the pro-life cause has always been essential to her belief, and there is a history of Democrat support against abortion. In the 60's and throughout the 70's, the Democratic Party was home to many Roman Catholics like Carol. And these Democrats brought their social conservatism with them. In the 80's, Reagan was able to peel off many Catholic votes like Carol's through his opposition to abortion. Many of these Democrats became known as "Reagan Democrats." As Carol got older, she became more conservative and told me that this is part of an evolutionary trend. It is called maturity. Today, Mrs. Golden is a retired media assistant from a local high school, baby sit her granddaughters, works on remodeling her home, spends quality time with her husband of 34 years, and in her free time edits my conservative tomes.

Carol finds that the Internet "has allowed conservatives to finally have a venue in which to learn the truth and have a voice." The mainstream media is dominated by a liberal mindset that has long considered itself the moderator of America's thought. Cable, Radio and the Internet over the past two decades have managed to erode the liberal advantage in the media. Interesting enough, most surveys show that when it comes to newsgathering outside network television is the purview of conservatives and libertarians. Conservatives and libertarians listen to a wider variety of news sources than many liberals and this has created new markets in the news arena. Rush Limbaugh dominates the national talk show during the afternoon with Sean Hannity and others like them following close on his heels, and the Internet has seen a plethora of websites dominated by either libertarians or conservatives. These voices are doing an end round around the mainstream media and providing new voices for debates on the major issues. While most Americans get their news from the big three, their impact is starting to erode. The Internet and talk radio resembles European media more. In England, the media is evenly divided between the right and left and opinions are as much a part of the front page as the editorial sections. The mainstream media is not a captive of one voice with the exception of the BBC, a government run agency. The Internet, using witty rhetoric and linking to appropriate sites, provides a useful counter to the more established media sources. These voices resonate new ideas and views, while enlivening the debate. Voices like Michele are part of the new opinion makers, never boring and always lively.

3

The Final Word

Michele Catalano is a wife with two children living in Long Island. During the Gulf War II, Ms. Catalano began a website strictly dedicated to news coverage of the Gulf War and this site proved to be the most updated site during the entire conflict. After the fighting concluded, she maintained and expanded the site. In addition to running her own website, working and running a family, she now runs the website, The Command Post, which not only includes news from Iraq but North Korea and the overall war on terror. What Ms. Catalano demonstrated is the power of the American conservative movement. American conservatism is the most radical force in the world. It is the force that totalitarians fear and it is the force that sends tremors through the halls of Europe for American conservatism is not conservatism in the traditional sense. While American conservatives defend certain traditions, they are not wed to them. During the recent court case dealing with Texas Sodomy laws, there were many conservatives who simply came out for the *legislative elimination of those laws based on protecting individual liberties.* What concerned many conservatives was the use of the courts to overturn a decision that rightly belongs in legislative hands. It is an over reach for the courts to meddle in affairs better left in the legislative prerogative. Roe v. Wade overturned 50 state laws, including the more liberal laws that were enacted. By basically ignoring the constitution, the courts set up a judicial civil war and undermined the courts neutrality in the legislative process.

The Wall Street Journal editorialized, "Our own view is that state anti-sodomy laws are almost never enforced, and they deserve the oblivion for which they are undoubtedly headed. But the issue is best settled democratically, not by judicial fiat, and that means it has to be discussable in the public square. Had abortion been left to legislatures in the 1970's we would have long ago settled the issue with a democratic compromise and spared our politics 30 years of cultural rancor and polarization." Institutions do matter to American conservatives, for these private institutions from the local church to the local charities are the "little platoons" that provide both hope and aid in time of stress. These "little platoons" are the neighbors whose knowledge of the local vicinity contribute to the well being of communities. Institutions maintain the fabric of society and the importance of an impartial judiciary allows freedom to reign and liberties to be protected. When the courts act in arbitrary methods, liberty itself is in peril, subject to constant changes by those who sit in the judicial seats.

Conservatives are the biggest defenders of free markets, and free markets are about change. To stand for free markets is to defend change on a daily basis for the consumer drives it. What conservatives' distrust is change instituted from above, from government. Conservatives accept the idea that government serves the people and was established to protect the rights of the individual. When government becomes too big, it becomes a threat to individual rights.

There is no secret to what creates wealth. Free markets, an impartial judicial system, limited government all conspire to create wealth. So why do we continue to debate the issues? A friend of mine told me that democracy gets in trouble once the voters' figure out that they can vote themselves gifts. Most politicians get elected on promises that can only be kept by taking from one sector of the population and giving to another. Power is based on providing selected interest groups a key to the federal treasury. Most politicians think about the next elections and not often on the long-term consequences of their actions.

William Greider of the Nation wrote, "The movement's grand ambition—one can no longer say grandiose—is to roll back the twentieth century, quite literally. That is, defenestrate the federal government and reduce its scale and powers to a level well below what it was before the New Deal's centralization. The primacy of private property rights is re-established over the shared public priorities expressed in government regulation. Above all, private wealth—both enterprises and individuals with higher incomes—are permanently insulated from the progressive claims of the graduated income tax." What Greider fails to understand is that by supporting the market system, the American conservative is the true radical. It is the capitalist who changes the way we view the world and it is through the efforts of the entrepreneur that progress and prosperity is created. The status quo is crushed and a new hierarchy is created if only for a short time until a new hierarchy rises to take over. The modern day socialist views himself as the agent of change, but he is the mere protector of the status quo, whereas the capitalist is forcing changes on society on a daily basis.

Ms. Camile Paglia wrote Capitalism is the same side of the coin as art. "Capitalist products are another version of the art works flooding western culture. The portable framed painting appeared at the birth of modern commerce in the early Renaissance. Capitalism and art have challenged and nourished each other ever since." Popular culture, including Rock and Roll, could only exist in a free market society. Capitalism featuring the gaudy and the greedy has been part of Western culture from the very beginning, and as Paglia notes, "It is the mysticism and glamour of things, which take on a personality of their own....Brand names are territorial cells of western identity. Our shiny chrome automobiles, like our armies of grocery boxes and cans, are extrapolations of hard, impermeable western personality."

Capitalism and art both threaten the basis of civilization. Capitalism, because entrepreneurs are always challenging the status quo, and art, because it challenges the way we look at the world. Art is guerrilla warfare with society and the most effective guerrilla fighter in Camille Paglia's mind is the poet Emily Dickinson, the American Sade. Paglia summarizes Dickinson's first subject is "power, psychological, natural, and divine, to which women freely access only in eras of earth-cult." Dickinson once wrote to a friend whose house burned down, "Dear friend, I congratulate you. Disaster endears beyond fortune." As Ms. Paglia observed about Emily Dickinson, "victimization means canonization in her Sadean cosmos." Paglia is curious about the lack of Christian compassion in many of Dickinson's personal letters to friends or relatives dealing with life crises such as death. Dickinson's stoic attitude is directly related to the paganism of our culture and in direct opposition to Christian compassion.

It is for this reason that American conservatives by promoting market economy are the true radicals. I do not view myself as conservative in the traditional sense, for change is the true engine of progress. A conservative, American style, is really an old fashioned liberal. As I have previously mentioned, there was a time in American History that to be a liberal was to be for less government, open trade and more freedom. Grover Cleveland was the last Democrat elected committed to smaller government and lower taxes. He was opposed to imperialism and foreign entanglements but was not afraid to stand up for American interests, when it was called for. He was the last of the Jeffersonian Democrats and soon the Democratic Party would retreat from its own past and evolve into the party of big government. Greider feels that the right is angling for a return to William McKinley, but in reality, the American conservative is more akin to the Jeffersonian vision of government.

It is the left who fears change and for good reason. As Michele Catalano demonstrated, Americans by nature are not going to be restrained by obstacles but look for obstacles to conquer. She was not going to depend upon the mainstream media to develop the latest but instead develop her own site. She became a rival news service to the mainstream media and she merely expanded the amount of information gathered. All by the simple use of computer keys, she held in her hands all of the world's information. Information is power and she used the power. American conservatives do not fear the future, they are the forces shaping it.

About the Author

Tom Donelson has enjoyed nearly a quarter century of writing various columns on issues ranging from economics and foreign affairs to sporting events. As an author, he has authored four other books, *Economics 101 And Other Thoughts, Viewing Boxing From Ringside, More Tales From Ringside* (Co-Authored with Frank Lotierzo) and Coming of Age: Andy Roddick Breakthrough Year (co-authored with Bethany Donelson)

Over the last two decades, Tom has given numerous lectures on public policy and currently acts as a consultant and writer in addition to running his over publishing company, Donelson Research and Publishing.

0-595-30589-X